SHAY SHULL

HARVEST HOUSE PUBLISHERS
EUGENE, OREGON

Mix-and-Match Cakes

Copyright © 2016 Mix and Match Mama
Published by Harvest House Publishers
Eugene, Oregon 97402
www.harvesthousepublishers.com

978-0-7369-6609-2

Cover and interior design by Faceout Studio
   Cover photos © Foodcollection / Getty; Rawpixel, ConstantinosZ, VikaRayu /
   Shutterstock; Anna Williams / Offset
Published in association with William K. Jensen Literary Agency,
   119 Bampton Court, Eugene, Oregon 97404

Printed in China

15 16 17 18 19 20 21 22 23 / DS-FO / 10 9 8 7 6 5 4 3 2 1

To Kensington
who helped me bake every
one of these cakes.

I love you, sweet girl!

CONTENTS

INTRODUCTION

Hi! I'm Shay, and I'm a foodie. It's nothing new. I've been baking and cooking since the fourth grade, so that's over 20 years of being in the kitchen. I used to think desserts were only good if they came from scratch. Then one day, I tried my friend Rachel New's chocolate chip pound cake and realized you can get a moist, delicious dessert starting with a boxed mix.

Everyone around me loved Rachel's cake. All my girlfriends requested the recipe, and over a period of time, we all started making it for every party and occasion. After a while, I started thinking. If I mixed and matched the main ingredients, I could create a whole new cake using the same method and producing the same yummy results.

After creating about 20 different versions of the Rachel New cake—each one delectable and different—Rachel joked that I could probably make a different version for every week of the year. *Hmm*, I thought. *I bet I could. I bet I could make a hundred.* Thus, my blog was born.

As a mom of three small kids, I don't have time to stay in the kitchen all day making desserts from scratch, so I'm going to let some boxed mixes help me. With a little imagination, we'll create a multitude of desserts for the entire year. It's more about the method than the recipe. Enjoy!

These recipes were designed for standard Bundt cake pans.
To use a different pan, consult the following chart:

PAN SIZE	COOKING TIME
9x13 baking pan	30 to 32 minutes
two 8-inch round cake pans	30 to 32 minutes
cupcakes (yield: 2 dozen)	15 to 18 minutes
mini Bundt cake pans (yield: 1 dozen)	16 to 18 minutes

THE ORIGINAL CHOCOLATE CHIP

INGREDIENTS

1 box yellow cake mix
1 small box instant vanilla pudding
1 small box instant chocolate pudding
$^1/_2$ cup vegetable oil
1 $^1/_4$ cups water
4 eggs
1 cup semisweet chocolate chips
powdered sugar for dusting

Where it all got started.

Preheat oven to 350° and grease a 10-inch Bundt pan. In mixing bowl, combine cake mix, puddings, oil, water, and eggs with electric mixer. Add in chocolate chips. Pour into prepared Bundt pan. Bake 40-45 minutes, or until toothpick inserted comes out clean. Let cake rest on counter in pan 10 minutes. Invert cake onto serving plate to finish cooling. Top with powdered sugar.

Spring

FRESH BLUEBERRY

INGREDIENTS

1 box white cake mix
2 small boxes instant vanilla pudding
$^1/_2$ cup vegetable oil
$1^1/_4$ cups water
4 eggs
1 cup fresh blueberries tossed with
   2 tablespoons flour
2 cups powdered sugar
1 tablespoon milk
1 lemon, juice plus zest, divided

*You know how I love a Bundt cake
that can double as breakfast.
Fresh blueberries in my cake?
Practically health food!
The little bit of **lemon in the glaze**
complements the cake beautifully.
You'll love this any time of day.*

Preheat oven to 350° and grease a 10-inch Bundt pan. In mixing bowl, combine cake mix, puddings, oil, water, and eggs with electric mixer. Stir in two tablespoons lemon juice and zest of half your lemon. Stir in blueberries that have been tossed with flour. (The flour prevents the blueberries from sinking to the bottom of your cake and keeps them evenly dispersed in your Bundt cake.) Pour into prepared pan and bake 40-45 minutes, or until toothpick inserted comes out clean. Let cake rest on counter in pan 10 minutes. Invert cake onto serving plate to finish cooling.

To make the glaze, combine powdered sugar with remaining 2 tablespoons lemon juice, remaining lemon zest, and milk. Add more powdered sugar if your glaze is too runny or more milk if it's too thick. Spoon over cooled cake.

CHOCOLATE CHERRY COCA-COLA

*If you're not a fan of cherry just leave it out (I'll never know!) or if you have
Dr. Pepper, Pepsi, or root beer on hand, swap that for the
Coca-Cola—it will give you the same effect. I think you're going to like this!*

INGREDIENTS

1 box chocolate cake mix
1 small box instant vanilla pudding
1 small box instant chocolate pudding
$^1/_2$ cup vegetable oil
$1^1/_4$ cups Coca-Cola, plus an additional
     few splashes for the frosting
4 eggs
3 tablespoons grenadine, divided (optional)
4 cups powdered sugar
$^1/_2$ cup butter, softened
2 tablespoons unsweetened cocoa powder
1 tablespoon vanilla

Preheat oven to 350° and grease a 10-inch Bundt pan. In mixing bowl, combine cake mix, puddings, oil, Coca-Cola, eggs, and 2 tablespoons grenadine with electric mixer. Pour into prepared pan and bake 40-45 minutes, or until toothpick inserted comes out clean.

Let cake rest on counter in pan 10 minutes. Invert cake onto serving plate to finish cooling.

To make the frosting, beat butter with powdered sugar, cocoa powder, a few splashes of Coca-Cola, and the remaining tablespoon of grenadine until creamy. Stir in vanilla and spread on cooled cake.

ALMOND WITH STRAWBERRY JAM

*The jam on the inside is very subtle. It simply complements the cake and keeps
it extra moist. This cake isn't really about the jam—the jam is just
a nice side-kick. Share a piece with close friends!*

INGREDIENTS

1 box white cake mix
2 small boxes instant vanilla pudding
$\frac{1}{2}$ cup vegetable oil
$1\frac{1}{4}$ cups water
4 eggs
2 tablespoons almond extract, divided
$1\frac{1}{2}$ cups strawberry jam
4 cups powdered sugar
$\frac{1}{2}$ cup butter, softened
3-4 splashes of milk
slivered almonds to garnish

Preheat oven to 350° and grease a 10-inch Bundt pan. In mixing bowl, combine cake mix, puddings, oil, water, and eggs with electric mixer. Stir in one tablespoon almond extract. Pour half the batter into prepared pan, take your jam, and spread it over the batter in the pan. Pour remaining half of the batter over jam and bake 40-45 minutes, or until toothpick inserted comes out clean. Let cake rest on counter in pan 10 minutes. Invert cake onto serving plate to finish cooling.

To make the frosting, beat butter with powdered sugar and milk until creamy. Stir in almond extract. Spread on cooled cake and top with slivered almonds.

OREO

INGREDIENTS

1 box chocolate cake mix
2 small boxes instant chocolate pudding
$\frac{1}{2}$ cup vegetable oil
$1\frac{1}{4}$ cups water
4 eggs
1 container vanilla frosting
16 Oreos

What's better than an Oreo? A chocolate cake with frosting and Oreos. Grab a big glass of milk and enjoy!

Preheat oven to 350° and grease a 10-inch Bundt pan or 12 mini Bundt pans.

In mixing bowl, combine cake mix, puddings, oil, water, and eggs with an electric mixer. Pour into prepared Bundt pan. Bake 40-45 minutes for a large cake or 16-18 minutes for mini cakes, or until toothpick inserted comes out clean. Let cake rest on counter in pan 10 minutes. Invert cake onto serving plate to finish cooling.

While the cake is cooling, empty your container of vanilla frosting into a mixing bowl. Crush about 10 Oreos and add to your frosting. (I put my Oreos in a large Ziploc bag and crush them with a rolling pin.) Then, crush about 6 more Oreos and keep to the side for garnish.

Frost your cake(s) with your Oreo frosting and garnish with remaining crushed Oreos.

ITALIAN CREAM

After over 20 years of baking, I've learned one valuable lesson: People are passionate about their love or their hatred of coconut. They are either madly in love with it or they think it's absolutely vile in any recipe. I personally think it's fantastic.

INGREDIENTS

1 box yellow cake mix
1 small box instant vanilla pudding
1 small box instant coconut pudding (use a
   second vanilla if you can't find coconut)
$^1/_2$ cup vegetable oil
$1^1/_4$ cups water
4 eggs
2 cups sweetened flaked coconut, divided
$1^1/_2$ cups chopped walnuts, divided
1 container cream cheese frosting

Preheat oven to 350° and grease a 10-inch Bundt pan. In mixing bowl, combine cake mix, puddings, oil, water, and eggs with electric mixer. Stir in one cup coconut and $^3/_4$ cup walnuts. Pour into prepared pan and bake 40-45 minutes, or until toothpick inserted comes out clean. Let cake rest on counter in pan 10 minutes. Invert cake onto serving plate to finish cooling.

To make the frosting, pour container of frosting in a bowl. Add in the remaining cup coconut and remaining $^3/_4$ cup walnuts and stir. Frost cooled cake.

No.
7

NUTELLA

Nutella is this wonderful chocolate-hazelnut spread that has the texture of peanut butter but tastes like chocolate. In Paris, they serve Nutella on warm crepes, in Amsterdam on pancakes, and in Rome on ice cream. My kids often have it on waffles instead of syrup...and I always snag a bite or two.

INGREDIENTS

1 box chocolate cake mix
2 small boxes instant chocolate pudding
$^{1}/_{2}$ cup vegetable oil
$1^{1}/_{4}$ cups water
4 eggs
$1^{1}/_{2}$ cups Nutella, divided
4 cups powdered sugar
$^{1}/_{2}$ cup butter, softened
3-4 splashes of milk

Preheat oven to 350° and grease a 10-inch Bundt pan. In mixing bowl, combine cake mix, puddings, oil, water, and eggs with electric mixer. Then mix in $^{3}/_{4}$ cup Nutella. Pour into prepared pan and bake 40-45 minutes, or until toothpick inserted comes out clean. Let cake rest on counter in pan 10 minutes. Invert the cake onto a serving plate to finish cooling.

To make the frosting, combine powdered sugar, butter, milk, and remaining $^{3}/_{4}$ cup Nutella with electric mixer until creamy. Spread on cooled cake.

·• seventeen ••

CRUNCHY PRETZEL

INGREDIENTS

1 box white cake mix
2 small boxes instant vanilla pudding
$^1/_2$ cup vegetable oil
$1^1/_4$ cups water
4 eggs
1 container vanilla frosting
2 cups pretzels, crushed
2 cups M&Ms

There are few things I like better than a salty-sweet combination. A little texture, crunch, salty, and sweet. My kids love this cake—I can't keep little hands out of the pretzel-M&M frosting!

Preheat oven to 350° and grease a 10-inch Bundt pan or 12 mini Bundt pans.

In mixing bowl, combine cake mix, puddings, oil, water, and eggs with electric mixer. Pour into prepared Bundt pan. Bake 40-45 minutes for a large cake or 16-18 minutes for mini cakes, or until toothpick inserted comes out clean. Let cake rest on counter in pan 10 minutes. Invert cake onto serving plate to finish cooling.

To make the frosting, scoop store-bought vanilla frosting into a bowl. Stir $1^1/_2$ cups of pretzel bits and $1^1/_2$ cups of M&Ms into the frosting. Frost over cooled cake and garnish with remaining pretzels and M&Ms.

COCONUT

If you love coconut, this is the cake for you!
It's super moist, super light, and just tastes like spring in a cake.

INGREDIENTS

1 box white cake mix
2 small boxes instant coconut pudding
   (substitute vanilla if you can't find coconut)
$\frac{1}{2}$ cup vegetable oil
$1\frac{1}{4}$ cups water
4 eggs
4 cups sweetened flaked coconut, divided
1 small can sweetened condensed milk
1 container vanilla frosting

Preheat oven to 350° and grease a 10-inch Bundt pan. In mixing bowl, combine cake mix, puddings, oil, water, and eggs with electric mixer. Stir in two cups coconut. Pour into prepared pan and bake 40-45 minutes, or until toothpick inserted comes out clean. Let cake rest on counter in pan 10 minutes. Invert the cake onto a serving plate.

While cake is still warm, take a fork and poke holes all across the top. Pour about half the can of sweetened condensed milk over the top of the cake (it will seep into the holes and make a great glaze for the top). Let the cake finish cooling.

To make the frosting, combine the vanilla frosting with $1\frac{1}{2}$ cups of coconut. Spread on cooled cake and then garnish with remaining $\frac{1}{2}$ cup coconut.

PEANUT BUTTER AND BANANA

You know what's awesome about this Bundt cake? Peanut butter plus a banana totally makes it healthy! That means you can eat two pieces (or even three!).

INGREDIENTS

1 box yellow cake mix
2 small boxes instant banana pudding
$\frac{1}{2}$ cup vegetable oil
$1\frac{1}{4}$ cups water
4 eggs
1 cup mashed bananas (about 2 bananas)
$1\frac{1}{2}$ cups peanut butter, divided
3 cups powdered sugar
$\frac{1}{2}$ cup butter, softened
3-4 splashes milk

Preheat oven to 350° and grease a 10-inch Bundt pan. In mixing bowl, combine cake mix, puddings, oil, water, and eggs with electric mixer. Beat in mashed bananas and $\frac{3}{4}$ cup peanut butter. Pour batter into prepared pan and bake 40-45 minutes, or until toothpick inserted comes out clean. Let cake rest on counter in pan 10 minutes. Invert the cake onto a serving plate to finish cooling.

To make the frosting, combine powdered sugar, softened butter, and milk with an electric mixer. Beat in remaining $\frac{3}{4}$ cup peanut butter. Add more powdered sugar if it's too runny and more milk if it's too thick. Frost cooled cake.

BANANAS FOSTER

INGREDIENTS

½ cup butter, softened and divided into slices
1 cup brown sugar
1 tablespoon rum extract
2 bananas, sliced
½ cup chopped pecans, toasted
1 box yellow cake mix
2 small boxes instant vanilla pudding
½ cup vegetable oil
1¼ cups water
4 eggs

This cake is my tribute to my husband's very favorite dessert. It might sound kind of complicated but it's really very simple. The brown sugar mixture makes a delicious glaze over the top of the cake.

Preheat oven to 350° and grease a 10-inch Bundt pan. In your prepared Bundt pan, drop slices of butter all around bottom. Put Bundt pan in the hot oven for 4-5 minutes, or until all the butter is melted. Remove pan from oven. Crumble brown sugar over the melted butter in the hot pan. Drizzle rum extract over butter/brown sugar mixture. Place sliced bananas over brown sugar mixture. Sprinkle pecans on top. Set aside and prepare cake mix.

In mixing bowl, combine cake mix, puddings, oil, water, and eggs with electric mixer. Pour into prepared pan slowly on top of banana/brown sugar mixture and bake 40-45 minutes, or until toothpick inserted comes out clean. Let cake rest on counter in pan 10 minutes. Invert the cake onto a serving plate. Let the cake finish cooling.

LEMON

INGREDIENTS

1 box lemon cake mix
1 small box instant vanilla pudding
1 small box instant lemon pudding
1/2 cup vegetable oil
1 cup water
1/4 cup lemon juice
4 eggs
2 cups powdered sugar
1 lemon, juice plus zest, divided

This cake is very lemony.
Using a box of vanilla pudding keeps
it from becoming too tart.

Preheat oven to 350° and grease a 10-inch Bundt pan. In mixing bowl, combine cake mix, puddings, oil, water, 1/4 cup lemon juice, and eggs with electric mixer. Pour into prepared pan and bake 40-45 minutes, or until toothpick inserted comes out clean. Let cake rest on counter in pan 10 minutes. Invert cake onto serving plate to finish cooling.

To make the glaze, combine powdered sugar with the zest and juice of one lemon. Mix together and spoon over cooled cake.

HUMMINGBIRD

If you're from the South, you know what hummingbird cake is. If you're not, you need to find out! It's a super moist yellow cake combined with bananas, pineapple, and pecans. It's heaven on a plate. Just one bite will make you feel like a Southern girl.

INGREDIENTS

1½ cups pecan pieces, toasted and divided
1 box yellow cake mix
2 small boxes instant vanilla pudding
½ cup vegetable oil
¾ cup water
4 eggs
2 bananas, mashed
1 8-oz can crushed pineapple (do not drain)
1 container cream cheese frosting

Preheat oven to 350° and grease a 10-inch Bundt pan. In mixing bowl, combine cake mix, puddings, oil, water, and eggs with electric mixer. Mix in mashed bananas. Stir in pineapple and juice. In the bottom of your Bundt pan, sprinkle ¾ cup pecans over the bottom. Pour cake batter into prepared pan over pecans and bake 40-45 minutes, or until toothpick inserted comes out clean. Let cake rest on counter in pan 10 minutes. Invert the cake onto a serving plate.

Spread frosting on top of cooled cake and top with remaining pecan pieces.

CHOCOLATE COCONUT

This cake is for all of you chocolate and coconut fans out there!

INGREDIENTS

1 box German chocolate cake mix
1 small box instant chocolate pudding
1 small box instant coconut pudding (or use another chocolate if you can't find coconut)
$\frac{1}{2}$ cup vegetable oil
$1\frac{1}{4}$ cups water
4 eggs
$\frac{1}{2}$ cup chocolate chips
1 14-oz. can sweetened condensed milk
3 egg yolks, slightly beaten
$\frac{1}{2}$ cup butter
1 teaspoon vanilla extract
1 $\frac{1}{3}$ cups sweetened coconut flakes

Preheat oven to 350° and grease a 10-inch Bundt pan. In mixing bowl, combine cake mix, puddings, oil, water, and eggs with electric mixer. Stir in chocolate chips. Pour into prepared Bundt pan. Bake 40-45 minutes, or until toothpick inserted comes out clean. Let cake rest on counter in pan 10 minutes. Invert cake onto serving plate to finish cooling.

Once cake is cool, stir together sweetened condensed milk, egg yolks, and butter in medium saucepan. Cook over low heat, stirring constantly, until mixture is thickened and bubbly. Remove from heat; stir in vanilla and coconut. Cool to room temperature. Spread over cooled cake.

LEMON COOKIE CRUNCH

INGREDIENTS

1 box lemon cake mix
2 small boxes instant lemon pudding (use vanilla if you can't find lemon)
$\frac{1}{2}$ cup vegetable oil
$1\frac{1}{4}$ cups water
4 eggs
1 container vanilla frosting
16 Golden Oreos
1 tablespoon lemon zest

The vanilla frosting has just a hint of lemon from your zest, and all those Golden Oreos make it extra delicious!

Preheat oven to 350° and grease a 10-inch Bundt pan. In mixing bowl, combine cake mix, puddings, oil, water, and eggs with an electric mixer. Pour into prepared Bundt pan.

Bake 40-45 minutes, or until toothpick inserted comes out clean. Let cake rest on counter in pan 10 minutes. Invert cake onto serving plate to finish cooling.

While the cake is cooling, empty your vanilla frosting into a mixing bowl. Crush 10 Golden Oreos and add to your frosting. (I put my Oreos in a large Ziploc bag and crush them with a rolling pin.) Stir in lemon zest. Crush 6 more Oreos and keep to the side for garnish.

Frost your cake with your Golden Oreo frosting and garnish with remaining crushed Oreos.

Summer

CHERRY LIMEADE

INGREDIENTS

- 1 box white cake mix
- 2 small boxes instant vanilla pudding
- 1/2 cup vegetable oil
- 1 container limeade concentrate, thawed and divided
- 1/2 cup grenadine or cherry juice, divided
- 4 eggs
- 2 cups powdered sugar

One of my favorite drinks is a cherry limeade. On the hot days of summer (all 200 of them in Texas!), you have to indulge in a cold drink to cool you down. I combined my favorite cold drink with my favorite little cake recipe. So refreshing and light!

Preheat oven to 350° and grease a 10-inch Bundt pan. In mixing bowl, combine cake mix, puddings, oil, 1 1/4 cups limeade concentrate, 2 tablespoons grenadine, and eggs with electric mixer. Pour cake batter into prepared pan and bake 40-45 minutes, or until toothpick inserted comes out clean. Let cake rest on counter in pan 10 minutes. Invert the cake onto a serving plate.

To make the glaze, combine powdered sugar with splashes of reserved limeade and grenadine. Combine until you get the right consistency. Add more powdered sugar if it's too thin and more limeade if it's too thick. Spoon glaze over cooled cake.

PIÑA COLADA

This pineapple-coconut cake will make you
feel like you're on vacation— it's like taking a bite out of Hawaii.

INGREDIENTS

1 box yellow cake mix
2 small boxes instant vanilla pudding
½ cup vegetable oil
¾ cup water
4 eggs
1 8-oz. can crushed pineapple (do not drain)
2 cups sweetened flaked coconut, divided
1 container vanilla frosting
1 cup Cool Whip
1 teaspoon rum extract

Preheat oven to 350° and grease a 10-inch Bundt pan. In mixing bowl, combine cake mix, puddings, oil, water, and eggs with electric mixer. Stir in pineapple (with juice!) and 1 cup coconut. Pour cake batter into prepared pan and bake 40-45 minutes, or until toothpick inserted comes out clean. Let cake rest on counter in pan 10 minutes. Invert the cake onto a serving plate.

To make the frosting, combine store-bought frosting with Cool Whip. Stir in remaining cup coconut and rum extract. Spread on cooled cake.

DR. PEPPER

This yummy chocolate cake uses Dr. Pepper instead of water. The chocolate and sweet soda pair beautifully together. Don't use diet—use the real thing! This cake (and especially frosting) will knock your socks off...or maybe your flip-flops off!

INGREDIENTS

1 box chocolate cake mix
2 small boxes instant chocolate pudding
1/2 cup vegetable oil
2 cups Dr. Pepper, divided
4 eggs
1 cup chocolate chips
4 cups powdered sugar
1/4 cup unsweetened cocoa powder
1/2 cup butter, softened

Preheat oven to 350° and grease a 10-inch Bundt pan. In mixing bowl, combine cake mix, puddings, oil, 1 1/4 cups Dr. Pepper, and eggs with electric mixer. Stir in chocolate chips. Pour batter into prepared pan and bake 40-45 minutes, or until toothpick inserted comes out clean. Let cake rest on counter in pan 10 minutes. Invert cake onto serving plate to finish cooling.

To make the frosting, beat butter with powdered sugar, cocoa powder, and a few splashes of Dr. Pepper. Spread on cooled cake.

PINK LEMONADE

INGREDIENTS

1 box white cake mix
2 small boxes instant lemon pudding
½ cup vegetable oil
2 cups thawed pink lemonade
   concentrate, divided
4 eggs
1 cup store-bought vanilla frosting
1 cup Cool Whip
pink sprinkles to garnish
pink food coloring, optional

It wouldn't be summer without pink lemonade, right? The key to this cake is to use thawed pink lemonade concentrate from the freezer section of the grocery store. It gives you that tart summer flavor. You'll come back to this cake all summer long.

Preheat oven to 350° and grease a 10-inch Bundt pan. In mixing bowl, combine cake mix, puddings, oil, 1¼ cups pink lemonade concentrate, and eggs with electric mixer. Pour into prepared Bundt pan and bake 40-45 minutes, or until toothpick inserted comes out clean. Let cake rest on counter in pan 10 minutes. Invert the cake onto a serving plate to finish cooling.

To make the frosting, combine frosting with Cool Whip in a mixing bowl. Stir in a few tablespoons of your remaining concentrate until you get your desired color. (Use a little pink food coloring if you like too.) Spread on cooled cake.

BLACKBERRY

This Father's Day, make a blackberry cake! You know me: If there's fruit in there, the cake qualifies as breakfast as well as dessert. Just give me a slice with a steaming cup of coffee and my morning is off to the perfect start.

INGREDIENTS

1 box white cake mix
2 small boxes instant vanilla pudding
$\frac{1}{2}$ cup vegetable oil
$1\frac{1}{4}$ cups water
4 eggs
1 cup frozen blackberries, thawed
$1\frac{1}{2}$ cups blackberry preserves
2 cups powdered sugar
1 lemon

Preheat oven to 350° and grease a 10-inch Bundt pan. In a mixing bowl, combine cake mix, puddings, oil, water, and eggs with electric mixer. Beat in thawed blackberries. Pour half of the batter into the prepared pan. Spoon preserves over batter all the way around and then top with the remaining half of your batter. Bake 40-45 minutes, or until toothpick inserted comes out clean. Let cake rest on counter in pan 10 minutes. Invert cake onto serving plate to finish cooling.

To make the glaze, combine powdered sugar with the juice of your lemon. Spoon over cooled cake.

BOSTON CREAM PIE

Boston cream pie is a yellow cake with yellow pudding inside and chocolate frosting outside. Really and truly, how can you not like that?

INGREDIENTS

1 box yellow cake mix
2 small boxes instant vanilla pudding
$^{1}/_{2}$ cup vegetable oil
$1^{1}/_{4}$ cups water
4 eggs
2 cups prepared vanilla pudding
1 container chocolate frosting

Preheat oven to 350° and grease a 10-inch Bundt pan. In a mixing bowl, combine cake mix, puddings, oil, water, and eggs with electric mixer. Pour batter into prepared pan and bake 40-45 minutes, or until toothpick inserted comes out clean. Let cake rest on counter in pan 10 minutes. Invert cake onto serving plate to finish cooling.

Once the cake is cool, take the handle end of a wooden spoon and poke holes around the top of the cake. Spoon pudding over the top of the cake and over the holes. Allow cake to sit in refrigerator at least one hour. Take the lid and foil off of your frosting and microwave 10-15 seconds. Remove cake from fridge and spoon chocolate frosting over the top of the vanilla pudding. Slice and serve.

PEACH

You can use one cup chopped fresh peaches or one cup chopped frozen peaches.
Either way you slice it, your cake is going to be delicious.
The almond glaze on top is the perfect match for the peach cake too.

INGREDIENTS

1 box white cake mix
2 small boxes instant vanilla pudding
½ cup vegetable oil
1¼ cups water
4 eggs
1 cup chopped fresh or frozen (thawed) peaches
2 cups powdered sugar
2-3 splashes of milk
2 teaspoons almond extract

Preheat oven to 350° and grease a 10-inch Bundt pan. In mixing bowl, combine cake mix, puddings, oil, water, and eggs with electric mixer. Stir in peaches. Pour into prepared pan and bake 40-45 minutes, or until toothpick inserted comes out clean. Let cake rest on counter in pan 10 minutes. Invert cake onto serving plate to finish cooling.

To make the glaze, combine powdered sugar with milk and extract and mix together with a spoon. Add more powdered sugar if your glaze is too runny or more milk if it's too thick. Spoon over cooled cake.

MARGARITA

*This cake is perfect for a girls night
on a summer evening!*

INGREDIENTS

1 box yellow cake mix
2 small boxes instant vanilla pudding
½ cup vegetable oil
2 cups prepared margarita mix, divided
4 eggs
4 cups powdered sugar
½ cup butter, softened
coarse salt or sprinkles to garnish

Preheat oven to 350° and grease a 10-inch Bundt pan. In mixing bowl, combine cake mix, puddings, oil, 1¼ cups margarita mix, and eggs with electric mixer. Pour into prepared pan and bake 40-45 minutes, or until toothpick inserted comes out clean. Let cake rest on counter in pan 10 minutes. Invert the cake onto a serving plate to finish cooling.

To make the frosting, combine powdered sugar, butter, and a few splashes of margarita mix with electric mixer until creamy. Spread on cooled cake. Garnish with salt or sugar sprinkles.

STRAWBERRY COCONUT

INGREDIENTS

- 1 box strawberry cake mix
- 2 small boxes instant coconut or vanilla pudding
- $\frac{1}{2}$ cup vegetable oil
- $1\frac{1}{4}$ cups water
- 4 eggs
- 2 cups shredded coconut, divided
- 1 container cream cheese frosting

This cake is like taking a bite out of summer. It's one of those desserts you'll make over and over again!

Preheat oven to 350° and grease a 10-inch Bundt pan. In mixing bowl, combine cake mix, puddings, oil, water, and eggs with electric mixer. Stir in one cup coconut. Pour into prepared pan and bake 40-45 minutes, or until toothpick inserted comes out clean. Let cake rest on counter in pan 10 minutes. Invert the cake onto a serving plate to finish cooling.

Take your store-bought cream cheese frosting and stir in remaining cup coconut. Frost cooled cake with coconut frosting.

CHOCOLATE ZUCCHINI

My daughter couldn't understand why anyone would add a vegetable to their cake.
When it was finished, she tried a bite, and then ate an entire piece. This girl is now
convinced that the best way to eat your veggies is in cake. I'll think you'll agree!

INGREDIENTS

1 box chocolate cake mix
1 small box instant vanilla pudding
1 small box instant chocolate pudding
$\frac{1}{2}$ cup vegetable oil
$1\frac{1}{4}$ cups water
4 eggs
2 tablespoons cinnamon, divided
1 cup zucchini, shredded
$\frac{1}{2}$ cup walnuts, chopped
1 cup semisweet chocolate chips
2 cups powdered sugar
2-3 splashes of milk

Preheat oven to 350° and grease a 10-inch Bundt pan. In mixing bowl, combine cake mix, puddings, oil, water, eggs, and $1\frac{1}{2}$ tablespoons cinnamon with electric mixer. Stir in zucchini, chocolate chips, and walnut pieces. Pour into prepared Bundt pan. Bake 40-45 minutes, or until toothpick inserted comes out clean. Let cake rest on counter in pan 10 minutes. Invert cake onto serving plate to finish cooling.

To make the glaze, combine powdered sugar and remaining $1\frac{1}{2}$ teaspoons of cinnamon with a few splashes of milk. Pour glaze over cooled cake.

STRAWBERRY LEMONADE

Nothing says summer like lemonade and strawberries!

INGREDIENTS

1 box white cake mix
2 small boxes instant lemon pudding
$\frac{1}{2}$ cup vegetable oil
1 cup water
$\frac{1}{4}$ cup frozen lemonade concentrate, thawed
    and undiluted
4 eggs
1 container vanilla frosting
$\frac{1}{2}$ cup Cool Whip
$\frac{1}{2}$ cup fresh strawberries, chopped

Preheat oven to 350° and grease a 10-inch Bundt pan. In mixing bowl, combine cake mix, puddings, oil, water, lemonade, and eggs with electric mixer. Pour into prepared pan and bake 40-45 minutes, or until toothpick inserted comes out clean. Let cake rest on counter in pan 10 minutes. Invert cake onto serving plate to finish cooling.

To make the frosting, spoon all of your store-bought vanilla frosting into a bowl. Fold in Cool Whip and strawberries. Using your hand mixer, combine the frosting mix just a second until the strawberries are incorporated into the frosting and it has a nice pink color (don't overmix or your frosting will become too thin). Spoon over cooled cake, slice, and enjoy.

MISSISSIPPI MUD

INGREDIENTS

1 box chocolate cake mix
2 small boxes instant chocolate pudding
½ cup vegetable oil
1¼ cups water
4 eggs
1 cup chocolate chips (plus more for garnish)
4 oz. cream cheese, softened (half a normal bar)
¼ cup butter, softened
1 7-oz. jar marshmallow cream
2 cups powdered sugar
1 teaspoon vanilla

*This is a moist chocolate cake
topped with a marshmallow
and cream cheese frosting.*
*This Texas gal was swooning over her
Mississippi Mud...and you will too!*

Preheat oven to 350° and grease a 10-inch Bundt pan. In mixing bowl, combine cake mix, puddings, oil, water, and eggs with electric mixer. Stir in one cup chocolate chips and pour into prepared Bundt pan. Bake 40-45 minutes, or until toothpick inserted comes out clean.

Let cake rest on counter in pan 10 minutes. Invert cake onto serving plate to finish cooling.

To make the frosting, beat cream cheese, butter, and marshmallow cream with powdered sugar until creamy. Beat in vanilla. Spread on cooled cake and top with a few chocolate chips.

DREAMSICLE

Dreamsicle, Orangesicle, Creamsicle...whatever you call it, it's that delicious creamy orange popsicle everyone loves on a hot summer day. It's orangey with a bit of vanilla cream inside—kind of retro and so delicious.

INGREDIENTS

1 box white cake mix
2 small boxes instant vanilla pudding
½ cup vegetable oil
¾ cup water
½ cup orange juice (plus a few tablespoons more if you're making your frosting from scratch)
4 eggs
1 cup white chocolate chips
2 tablespoons orange zest, divided
½ cup butter, softened
3 cups powdered sugar
orange food coloring, optional

Preheat oven to 350° and grease a 10-inch Bundt pan. In mixing bowl, combine cake mix, puddings, oil, water, ½ cup orange juice, and eggs with electric mixer. Stir in white chocolate chips and one tablespoon of orange zest. Pour into prepared pan and bake 40-45 minutes, or until toothpick inserted comes out clean. Let cake rest on counter in pan 10 minutes. Invert the cake onto a serving plate to finish cooling.

To make your frosting, beat butter, powdered sugar, and splashes of orange juice with an electric mixer. Add more juice if the frosting is too thick and more powdered sugar if it's too thin. Stir in remaining tablespoon of orange zest and a little orange food coloring. Frost your cooled cake.

BANANA CREAM PIE

This cake will delight even the pickiest eaters. Moist and delicious with cream cheese frosting...perfection on a plate.

INGREDIENTS

1 box yellow cake mix
2 small boxes instant banana pudding
$\frac{1}{2}$ cup vegetable oil
$1\frac{1}{4}$ cups water
4 eggs
1 cup mashed bananas (about 2 bananas)
3 cups powdered sugar
1 8-oz. package cream cheese, softened
3-4 splashes milk
crushed pieces of Nilla Wafers to garnish

Preheat oven to 350° and grease a 10-inch Bundt pan. In mixing bowl, combine cake mix, puddings, oil, water, and eggs with electric mixer. Beat in mashed up bananas. Pour batter into prepared pan and bake 40-45 minutes, or until toothpick inserted comes out clean.

Let cake rest on counter in pan 10 minutes. Invert the cake onto a serving plate to finish cooling.

To make the frosting, combine powdered sugar, softened cream cheese, and milk with an electric mixer. Beat until frosting reaches desired consistency. Add more powdered sugar if it's too runny and more milk if it's too thick. Frost cooled cake and top with crushed pieces of Nilla Wafer cookies.

FRUITY PEBBLES

INGREDIENTS

1 box white cake mix
2 small boxes instant vanilla pudding
$^1/_2$ cup vegetable oil
$1^1/_4$ cups water
4 eggs
3 cups Fruity Pebbles cereal, divided
1 container vanilla frosting

Let's get something straight here: I could probably do 101 Bundt cakes just using cereal. This method was so much fun! The Fruity Pebbles cereal made the cake taste like funfetti. It would also be good with Cocoa Pebbles and a chocolate cake mix. What combinations can you dream up?

Preheat oven to 350° and grease a 10-inch Bundt pan. In mixing bowl, combine cake mix, puddings, oil, water, and eggs with electric mixer. Stir in $1^1/_2$ cups Fruity Pebbles. Pour into prepared Bundt pan. Bake 40-45 minutes, or until toothpick inserted comes out clean. Let cake rest on counter in pan 10 minutes. Invert cake onto serving plate to finish cooling.

To make the frosting, stir one cup Fruity Pebbles cereal into your store-bought vanilla frosting. Frost cooled cake. Just before serving, sprinkle remaining $^1/_2$ cup Fruity Pebbles on top.

No. 31

ROOT BEER

My favorite soft drink is a good old-fashioned root beer. Add a scoop of ice cream to the side of this cake and you have yourself a root beer float. Well, sort of!

INGREDIENTS

1 box yellow cake mix
2 small boxes instant vanilla pudding
$\frac{1}{2}$ cup vegetable oil
2 cups root beer, divided
4 eggs
3 cups powdered sugar
$\frac{1}{2}$ cup butter, softened

Preheat oven to 350° and grease a 10-inch Bundt pan. In mixing bowl, combine cake mix, puddings, oil, 1$\frac{3}{4}$ cups root beer, and eggs with electric mixer. Pour batter into prepared pan and bake 40-45 minutes, or until toothpick inserted comes out clean. Let cake rest on counter in pan 10 minutes. Invert cake onto serving plate to finish cooling.

To make the frosting, beat butter with powdered sugar and remaining $\frac{1}{4}$ cup root beer. Add more powdered sugar if the icing is too thin and more root beer if it's too thick. Spread on cooled cake.

PINEAPPLE UPSIDE-DOWN

My kids love flipping over the pan to
reveal the pineapple topping.

INGREDIENTS

1 15-oz. can sliced pineapples (slice each
   pineapple ring in half), liquid reserved
1 box yellow cake mix
2 small boxes instant vanilla pudding
$^1/_2$ cup vegetable oil
$1^1/_4$ cups pineapple juice reserved
   from pineapples
4 eggs

Preheat oven to 350° and grease a 10-inch Bundt pan or 12 mini Bundt pans.

In a mixing bowl, combine cake mix, puddings, oil, pineapple juice, and eggs with electric mixer. Next, carefully place just one row of slices of pineapple along the bottom of the pan or if you are using mini pans, place one ring in each. *You will not use all of the pineapple!*

Carefully pour your cake batter on top of the pineapple in your Bundt pan and bake 40-45 minutes for a large cake or 16-18 minutes for mini cakes, or until toothpick inserted comes out clean. Let cake rest on counter in pan 10 minutes. Invert the cake onto a serving plate. Let the cake finish cooling.

Because there isn't a frosting, this cake is really quick to whip together. I buy the 15-oz. can of pineapple because I want as much juice as I can get for the batter. Reserve the extra pineapple for a separate recipe. If you find your can of pineapple doesn't give you as much juice as you need, just add water.

HAWAIIAN LUAU

INGREDIENTS

- 1 box coconut cake mix
- 2 small boxes instant coconut pudding (use vanilla if you can't find coconut)
- ½ cup vegetable oil
- 1 15-oz. can crushed pineapple (reserve the juice!), divided
- 1 cup pineapple juice from your canned pineapple
- ¼ cup water (or more pineapple juice if your can has any left)

- 4 eggs
- 1 container cream cheese frosting
- 2 cups sweetened, flaked coconut, divided
- Maraschino cherries to garnish (optional)

Even if you can't go to the islands, you can eat a cake that brings the island flavors to you. Aloha.

Preheat oven to 350° and grease a 10-inch Bundt pan. In mixing bowl, combine cake mix, puddings, oil, pineapple juice, water, and eggs with electric mixer. Stir in 1 cup crushed pineapple and one cup coconut. Pour into prepared pan and bake 40-45 minutes, or until toothpick inserted comes out clean. Let cake rest on counter in pan 10 minutes. Invert cake onto serving plate to finish cooling.

Stir remaining cup coconut into store-bought frosting and frost cooled cake. Top cake with cherries.

COCONUT LIME

Two of the most prominent flavors of the season come together in one cake!
This cake is light and fresh and perfect for summertime.

INGREDIENTS

1 box coconut cake mix
2 small boxes instant coconut pudding
   (use vanilla if you can't find coconut)
½ cup vegetable oil
1 cup water
¼ cup fresh lime juice for cake plus extra
   for frosting
4 tablespoons lime zest, divided
4 eggs
1 8-oz. package cream cheese, softened
4 cups powdered sugar
1 cup sweetened, flaked coconut

Preheat oven to 350° and grease a 10-inch Bundt pan. In mixing bowl, combine cake mix, puddings, oil, water, ¼ cup lime juice, and eggs with electric mixer. Stir in 2 tablespoons zest. Pour into prepared pan and bake 40-45 minutes, or until toothpick inserted comes out clean. Let cake rest on counter in pan 10 minutes. Invert cake onto serving plate to finish cooling.

Using an electric mixer, combine cream cheese and powdered sugar with a little more lime juice (2-3 tablespoons or so) until smooth. Add more powdered sugar if the frosting is too thin and more lime juice if it's too thick. Stir in remaining 2 tablespoons lime zest and coconut.

Spoon over cooled cake, garnish with a little more coconut, slice, and enjoy.

PEACH UPSIDE-DOWN

In Texas, June is peach month. Peaches are ripe, juicy, and delicious.

INGREDIENTS

$^1/_3$ cup butter, softened and divided into slices
$^3/_4$ cup brown sugar
1 15-oz. can sliced peaches, drained
1 box yellow cake mix
2 small boxes instant vanilla pudding
$^1/_2$ cup vegetable oil
$1^1/_4$ cups water
4 eggs

Preheat oven to 350° and grease a 10-inch Bundt pan. In your prepared Bundt pan, drop slices of butter all around bottom. Next, sprinkle brown sugar evenly over the butter all the way around the bottom of the Bundt pan. Put Bundt pan in the oven for 6 minutes.

Meanwhile, in a mixing bowl, combine cake mix, puddings, oil, water, and eggs with electric mixer. After you remove the Bundt pan from the oven, carefully place your peach slices along the bottom of the pan on top of your melted butter and sugar mixture. *You will not use all of the peaches!* Just place one row of slices in a ring around the pan.

Carefully pour your cake batter on top of the peaches in your Bundt pan and bake 40-45 minutes, or until toothpick inserted comes out clean. Let cake rest on counter in pan 10 minutes. Invert the cake onto a serving plate. Let the cake finish cooling.

HOT FUDGE SUNDAE

INGREDIENTS

1 box white cake mix
2 small boxes instant vanilla pudding
$^1/_2$ cup vegetable oil
$1^1/_4$ cups water
4 eggs
hot fudge, warmed in the microwave
    about a minute
whipped cream
sprinkles
cherries

*The perfect cake for a **celebration**.*

Preheat oven to 350° and grease a 10-inch Bundt pan or 12 mini Bundt pans.

In mixing bowl, combine cake mix, puddings, oil, water, and eggs with electric mixer. Pour into prepared pan and bake 40-45 minutes for a large cake or 16-18 minutes for mini cakes, or until toothpick inserted comes out clean. Let cake rest on counter in pan 10 minutes. Invert cake onto serving plate to finish cooling.

Once cake is cool, drizzle hot fudge on top, dollop with whipped cream, and add sprinkles and a cherry.

RAINBOW

*This cake is a **party** on a **plate**. My kids love helping me make it!*

INGREDIENTS

1 box white cake mix
2 small boxes instant vanilla pudding
½ cup vegetable oil
1¼ cups water
4 eggs
orange (or yellow), pink (or red), blue, green, and
   purple food coloring
1 container vanilla frosting
sprinkles

Preheat oven to 350° and grease a 10-inch Bundt pan. In mixing bowl, combine cake mix, puddings, oil, water, and eggs with electric mixer.

Separate your batter between 5 bowls (or 6 if you want to do 6 different colors) making sure that the bowls decrease in amount of batter as you go down. (Bowl #1 should have the most batter, bowl #2 a little less...all the way to bowl #5 with the smallest amount of batter).

Using your food coloring, color each bowl a different color. Stir well, making sure to incorporate the color throughout the batter.

Spread batter from bowl #1 evenly across the bottom of your prepared Bundt pan. Then spread batter from bowl #2 over the first layer. Repeat until all your batter has been used. Don't swirl them together. Bake 40-45 minutes, or until toothpick inserted comes out clean. Let cake rest on counter in pan 10 minutes. Invert cake onto serving plate to finish cooling.

Frost cooled cake with vanilla frosting and top with sprinkles.

KEY LIME

*I used key limes for this cake—they're little limes usually found in one-pound bags
next to the lemons and limes. If you can't find them, just substitute a
couple of regular limes. Key limes just have a particular taste that says summer.
You'll feel like you're in the Florida Keys when you eat this cake.*

INGREDIENTS

1 box white cake mix
2 small boxes instant vanilla pudding
$\frac{1}{2}$ cup vegetable oil
1 cup water
3 tablespoons key lime zest, divided
$\frac{1}{4}$ cup fresh key lime juice (about 10 key limes)
   plus juice from a few extra key limes for frosting
4 eggs
1 8-oz. package cream cheese, softened
4 cups powdered sugar

Preheat oven to 350° and grease a 10-inch Bundt pan. In mixing bowl, combine cake mix, puddings, oil, water, 1$\frac{1}{2}$ tablespoons zest, $\frac{1}{4}$ cup key lime juice, and eggs with electric mixer. Pour into prepared pan and bake 40-45 minutes, or until toothpick inserted comes out clean. Let cake rest on counter in pan 10 minutes. Invert cake onto serving plate to finish cooling.

Using an electric mixer, combine cream cheese and powdered sugar with a little more key lime juice (2-3 tablespoons or so) until smooth. Beat in remaining 1$\frac{1}{2}$ tablespoons key lime zest. Spoon over cooled cake, garnish with a little more zest, slice, and enjoy.

Fall

PUMPKIN SPICE LATTE

INGREDIENTS

1 box spice cake mix
2 small boxes instant vanilla pudding
½ cup vegetable oil
1¼ cups water
4 eggs
1 cup pumpkin
4 cups powdered sugar
½ cup butter, softened
3-4 splashes milk
2 tablespoons cinnamon

When asked to name my favorite of the 101 Bundt cakes, I always say this one. It is fall. And fall is my favorite time of year.

Preheat oven to 350° and grease a 10-inch Bundt pan. In mixing bowl, combine cake mix, puddings, oil, water, eggs, and pumpkin with an electric mixer. Pour into prepared Bundt pan. Bake 40-45 minutes, or until toothpick inserted comes out clean. Let cake rest on counter in pan 10 minutes. Invert cake onto serving plate to finish cooling.

In a small bowl, combine powdered sugar, butter, and milk with an electric mixer until creamy. Stir in cinnamon. Frost cooled cake.

BANANA NUT

This banana nut cake with brown sugar frosting
wins everyone over—even those who dislike nuts!

INGREDIENTS

1 box yellow cake mix
2 small boxes instant vanilla pudding
$^1/_2$ cup vegetable oil
$1^1/_4$ cups water
4 eggs
1 cup mashed bananas (about 2 bananas)
1 tablespoon cinnamon
1 cup chopped walnuts
4 cups powdered sugar
$^1/_2$ cup butter, softened
3-4 splashes milk
2 tablespoons brown sugar

Preheat oven to 350° and grease a 10-inch Bundt pan. In mixing bowl, combine cake mix, puddings, oil, water, and eggs with electric mixer. Beat in bananas and cinnamon. Stir in walnuts. Pour batter into prepared pan and bake 40-45 minutes, or until toothpick inserted comes out clean. Let cake rest on counter in pan 10 minutes. Invert the cake onto a serving plate. Let the cake finish cooling.

To make the frosting, combine powdered sugar, softened butter, milk, and brown sugar with an electric mixer in a bowl. Beat until frosting reaches desired consistency. Add more powdered sugar if it's too runny and more milk if it's too thick. Frost cooled cake. Slice and serve.

PEANUT BUTTER

This tastes just like a soft peanut butter cookie.
The only thing you need to go with it is a tall glass of milk.

INGREDIENTS

1 box yellow cake mix
2 small boxes instant vanilla pudding
$^1/_2$ cup vegetable oil
$1^1/_4$ cups water
4 eggs
$1^1/_2$ cups peanut butter, divided
$^1/_2$ cup butter, softened
4 cups powdered sugar
2-3 splashes of milk

Preheat oven to 350° and grease a 10-inch Bundt pan. In mixing bowl, combine cake mix, puddings, oil, water, and eggs with electric mixer. Beat in one cup peanut butter. Pour into prepared pan and bake 40-45 minutes, or until toothpick inserted comes out clean. Let cake rest on counter in pan 10 minutes. Invert cake onto serving plate to finish cooling.

To make the frosting, combine butter, powdered sugar, milk, and remaining $^1/_2$ cup peanut butter with an electric mixer. Add more sugar if the frosting is too runny and more milk if it's too thick. Spread frosting over cooled cake.

BUTTERSCOTCH

INGREDIENTS

1 box yellow cake mix
2 small boxes instant butterscotch pudding
$\frac{1}{2}$ cup vegetable oil
$1\frac{1}{4}$ cups water
4 eggs
$\frac{1}{2}$ cup butterscotch chips
1 container vanilla frosting
$\frac{1}{2}$ cup butterscotch ice cream topping

This was the first cake I mixed and matched from the original, so it's near and dear to my heart. It started them all, and it's delicious to boot!

Preheat oven to 350° and grease a 10-inch Bundt pan. In mixing bowl, combine cake mix, puddings, oil, water, and eggs with electric mixer. Add in butterscotch chips. Pour into prepared Bundt pan. Bake 40-45 minutes, or until toothpick inserted comes out clean. Let cake rest on counter in pan 10 minutes. Invert cake onto serving plate to finish cooling.

To make the frosting, stir your butterscotch topping right into your vanilla frosting, swirl together, and frost your cooled cake.

APPLE CINNAMON

This combination of apples, cinnamon, and yummy cream cheese frosting will have you thinking of fall!

INGREDIENTS

1 box yellow cake mix
2 small boxes instant vanilla pudding
½ cup vegetable oil
1 cup water
4 eggs
1 cup applesauce
2 tablespoons cinnamon (divided)
1 8-oz package cream cheese, softened
¼ cup butter, softened
4 cups powdered sugar
3-4 tablespoons milk
1 teaspoon vanilla

Preheat oven to 350° and grease a 10-inch Bundt pan or 12 mini Bundt pans.

In mixing bowl, combine cake mix, puddings, oil, water, eggs, applesauce, and 1 tablespoon cinnamon with electric mixer. Pour into prepared Bundt pan. Bake 40-45 minutes for one large cake or 16-18 minutes for mini cakes, or until toothpick inserted comes out clean. Let cake rest on counter in pan 10 minutes. Invert cake onto serving plate to finish cooling.

Once cake is cooled, combine remaining ingredients and the remaining tablespoon of cinnamon in mixing bowl. Beat with electric mixer. Drizzle over cooled cake.

CARAMEL

The frosting takes the cake!

INGREDIENTS

1 box yellow cake mix
2 small boxes instant vanilla pudding
$\frac{1}{2}$ cup vegetable oil
1 $\frac{1}{4}$ cups water
4 eggs
1 cup Caramel Bits
1 cup butter
2 cups packed brown sugar
$\frac{1}{2}$ cup milk
2 teaspoons vanilla
4 cups powdered sugar

Preheat oven to 350° and grease a 10-inch Bundt pan. In mixing bowl, combine cake mix, puddings, oil, water, and eggs with electric mixer. Add in Caramel Bits. Pour into prepared Bundt pan. Bake 40-45 minutes, or until toothpick inserted comes out clean. Let cake rest on counter in pan 10 minutes. Invert cake onto serving plate to finish cooling.

For the frosting, melt butter in saucepan over medium heat. Add brown sugar and bring to a boil, stirring constantly. Add in milk and bring back to a boil. Remove from heat and stir in vanilla. Let mixture cool to lukewarm (about 30 minutes). Whisk powdered sugar into butter mixture. Drizzle over cooled cake. Lick bowl...Trust me, you will!

CARAMEL APPLE CIDER

INGREDIENTS

- 1 box yellow cake mix
- 2 small boxes instant vanilla pudding
- ½ cup vegetable oil
- 1 cup apple cider, plus a few extra splashes for the frosting
- 4 eggs
- 1 cup applesauce
- 2 tablespoons cinnamon (divided)
- 1 cup caramel pieces (found on the chocolate chip aisle)

- 1 cup caramel ice cream topping
- ½ cup butter, softened
- 4 cups powdered sugar

My favorite fall drink
but in cake form.

Preheat oven to 350° and grease a 10-inch Bundt pan. In mixing bowl, combine cake mix, puddings, oil, 1 cup cider, eggs, applesauce, and 1 tablespoon cinnamon with electric mixer. Stir in caramel pieces. Pour into prepared Bundt pan. Bake 40-45 minutes, or until toothpick inserted comes out clean. Let cake rest on counter in pan 10 minutes. Invert cake onto serving plate to finish cooling.

To make the frosting, beat butter, powdered sugar, and 2-3 splashes of cider with electric mixer until creamy. Beat in remaining tablespoon of cinnamon. Add more sugar if the frosting is too runny and more cider if it's too thick. Spoon caramel ice cream topping over cooled cake and then frost with your cider frosting.

No. 46

DARK CHOCOLATE

Nothing says "I love chocolate"
more than dark chocolate!

INGREDIENTS

1 box chocolate fudge cake mix
2 small boxes instant chocolate fudge pudding
$^1/_2$ cup vegetable oil
$1^1/_4$ cups water
4 eggs
2 cups dark chocolate chips, divided
$^1/_2$ cup whipping cream

Preheat oven to 350° and grease a 10-inch Bundt pan. In mixing bowl, combine cake mix, puddings, oil, water, and eggs with electric mixer. Add in 1 cup dark chocolate chips. Pour into prepared Bundt pan. Bake 40-45 minutes, or until toothpick inserted comes out clean. Let cake rest on counter in pan 10 minutes. Invert cake onto serving plate to finish cooling.

To make the ganache, place remaining cup of chocolate chips in medium bowl. On stove, bring whipping cream just up to boiling. Pour over chocolate chips. Stir a few minutes until chocolate is melted. Let stand 15 minutes, stirring occasionally. Pour over cooled cake.

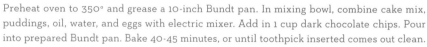

S'MORES

Can you picture yourself around the campfire?
I sure can. Here's to a toasty evening!

INGREDIENTS

1 box yellow cake mix
2 small boxes instant vanilla pudding
$^1/_2$ cup vegetable oil
$1^1/_4$ cups water
4 eggs
1 cup graham cracker crumbs (I pulse my
   graham crackers in the food processor but
   you could just put them in a baggie and roll a
   rolling pin over them.)
1 16-oz. jar hot fudge topping (not chocolate syrup)
1 7-oz. jar marshmallow cream
1 container whipped fluffy white frosting

Preheat oven to 350° and grease a 10-inch Bundt pan or 12 mini Bundt pans.

In mixing bowl, combine cake mix, puddings, oil, water, and eggs with electric mixer. Add in graham cracker crumbs and stir. Pour into prepared Bundt pan. Take your hot fudge sauce and drop it around the top of the cake (when you invert the cake, the fudge will be on the bottom). You don't need to spread it evenly, just drop big dollops all the way across. The fudge will spread by itself while baking.

Bake 40-45 minutes for a large cake or 16-18 minutes for mini cakes, or until toothpick inserted comes out clean. Let cake rest 10 minutes. Invert cake onto serving plate to finish cooling.

To make the frosting, combine marshmallow cream and frosting in a bowl. Spread over cooled cake.

TOFFEE CRUNCH

INGREDIENTS

1 box yellow cake mix
2 small boxes instant vanilla pudding
$^1/_2$ cup vegetable oil
$1^1/_4$ cups water
4 eggs
2 cups Heath Pieces, divided
1 container vanilla frosting
2 tablespoons brown sugar
regular sized Heath bars for garnish

I adore a little crunch with my cake, and this totally fits the bill. A toffee crunch cake with a brown sugar frosting!

Preheat oven to 350° and grease a 10-inch Bundt pan or 12 mini Bundt pans. In mixing bowl, combine cake mix, puddings, oil, water, and eggs with electric mixer. Stir in one cup Heath Pieces. Pour into prepared Bundt pan. Bake 40-45 minutes for a large cake or 16-18 minutes for mini cakes, or until toothpick inserted comes out clean. Let cake rest on counter in pan 10 minutes. Invert cake onto serving plate to finish cooling.

To make the frosting, stir brown sugar into store-bought vanilla frosting. Add one cup Heath Pieces to frosting. Frost each cake with icing. Top cake with chopped-up pieces of a regular sized Heath bar.

SNICKERDOODLE

*You could skip the frosting, dust with powdered sugar, and serve
this for breakfast on a cool fall morning.* **It's delicious with coffee!**

INGREDIENTS

1 box white cake mix
2 small boxes instant vanilla pudding
$\frac{1}{2}$ cup vegetable oil
$1\frac{1}{4}$ cups water
4 eggs
4 tablespoons cinnamon (divided)
$\frac{2}{3}$ cup butter, softened
4 cups powdered sugar
3-4 tablespoons milk
1 teaspoon vanilla

Preheat oven to 350° and grease a 10-inch Bundt pan. In mixing bowl, combine cake mix, puddings, oil, water, eggs, and 2 tablespoons cinnamon with electric mixer. Pour into prepared Bundt pan. Bake 40-45 minutes, or until toothpick inserted comes out clean. Let cake rest on counter in pan 10 minutes. Invert cake onto serving plate to finish cooling.

In a medium sized bowl, combine butter, powdered sugar, and milk with electric mixer until creamy. Add in vanilla and remaining 2 tablespoons of cinnamon. Frost cooled cake.

APPLE BUTTERSCOTCH

The praline crunch frosting really adds to the apple and butterscotch.

INGREDIENTS

1 box yellow cake mix
2 small boxes instant butterscotch pudding
$^1/_2$ cup vegetable oil
$1^1/_4$ cups water
4 eggs
1 cup grated apple (I peeled 2 Braeburns and then used the cheese grater to grate them up)
1 cup butterscotch chips
1 container vanilla frosting
$1^1/_2$ cups store-bought praline pecans (or you could get fancy and make them yourself)

Preheat oven to 350° and grease a 10-inch Bundt pan. In mixing bowl, combine cake mix, puddings, oil, water, and eggs with electric mixer. Stir in apple and butterscotch chips. Pour into prepared Bundt pan. Bake 40-45 minutes, or until toothpick inserted comes out clean. Let cake rest on counter in pan 10 minutes. Invert cake onto serving plate to finish cooling.

Roughly chop one cup of the praline pecans. Stir into vanilla frosting. Frost cooled cake and then top with the remaining $^1/_2$ cup of pecans.

CINNAMON ROLL

INGREDIENTS

1 box white cake mix
2 small boxes instant vanilla pudding
½ cup vegetable oil
1¼ cups water
4 eggs
4 tablespoons cinnamon (divided)
1 cup brown sugar
3 cups powdered sugar
3-4 tablespoons milk

Is there anything better than a cinnamon roll? This is one of those cakes that makes people scrape the bottom of the plate for extra icing. It's so good you'll want it for breakfast and dessert.

Preheat oven to 350° and grease a 10-inch Bundt pan. In mixing bowl, combine cake mix, puddings, oil, water, eggs, and 2 tablespoons cinnamon with electric mixer. Pour half of the batter into your prepared Bundt pan. In a small bowl, combine brown sugar and remaining 2 tablespoons cinnamon. Sprinkle brown sugar mixture over batter in pan. Pour remaining batter on top of brown sugar mixture. Bake 40-45 minutes, or until toothpick inserted comes out clean. Let cake rest on counter in pan 10 minutes. Invert cake onto serving plate to finish cooling.

In a small bowl, combine powdered sugar and milk to form a glaze. Add more powdered sugar if it's too runny and more milk if it's too thick. Drizzle glaze over cooled cake.

PUMPKIN

I just love pumpkin season!

INGREDIENTS

1 box yellow cake mix
2 small instant pumpkin puddings
½ cup vegetable oil
1 cup water
4 eggs
1 cup pumpkin
2 tablespoons cinnamon, divided
1 container cream cheese frosting

Preheat oven to 350° and grease a 10-inch Bundt pan. In mixing bowl, combine cake mix, puddings, oil, water, eggs, pumpkin, and 1 tablespoon cinnamon with an electric mixer. Pour into prepared Bundt pan. Bake 40-45 minutes, or until toothpick inserted comes out clean. Let cake rest on counter in pan 10 minutes. Invert cake onto serving plate to finish cooling.

Remove foil lid from frosting, microwave for 15 seconds (to get it really creamy), and stir in remaining tablespoon of cinnamon. Frost cooled cake.

CHOCOLATE SPICE

A fall cake doesn't always have to be pumpkin, right? All the chocolate lovers out there need a fall cake too. I can't think of a better combination— chocolate, cream cheese, and cinnamon.

INGREDIENTS

1 box chocolate cake mix
2 small boxes instant chocolate pudding
$\frac{1}{2}$ cup vegetable oil
$1\frac{1}{4}$ cups water
4 eggs
4 tablespoons cinnamon, divided
1 8-oz. package cream cheese, softened
4 cups powdered sugar
3-4 splashes milk

Preheat oven to 350° and grease a 10-inch Bundt pan. In mixing bowl, combine cake mix, puddings, oil, water, and eggs with electric mixer. Mix in 2 tablespoons of cinnamon. Pour into prepared Bundt pan. Bake 40-45 minutes, or until toothpick inserted comes out clean. Let cake rest on counter in pan 10 minutes. Invert cake onto serving plate to finish cooling.

To make the frosting, beat cream cheese with powdered sugar and milk until creamy. Beat in remaining 2 tablespoons of cinnamon. Spread on cooled cake.

No. 54

CHOCOLATE CARAMEL OATMEAL

INGREDIENTS

1 box yellow cake mix
2 small boxes instant vanilla pudding
$^1/_2$ cup vegetable oil
$1^1/_4$ cups water
4 eggs
2 tablespoons cinnamon
1 cup uncooked (not instant) oatmeal
1 cup chocolate chips
1 cup caramel ice cream topping
1 container vanilla frosting

Oatmeal is the surprise ingredient—and tasty, too!

Preheat oven to 350° and grease a 10-inch Bundt pan. In mixing bowl, combine cake mix, puddings, oil, water, eggs, and cinnamon with electric mixer. Stir in oatmeal and chocolate chips. Pour half of the batter into your prepared Bundt pan. Drizzle caramel over the batter. Pour remaining cake batter on top of the caramel layer. Bake 40-45 minutes, or until toothpick inserted comes out clean. Let cake rest on counter in pan 10 minutes. Invert cake onto serving plate to finish cooling. Spread vanilla frosting over cooled cake.

Winter

WINTER WHITE CHOCOLATE

INGREDIENTS

1 box white cake mix
2 small boxes instant vanilla pudding
$^1/_2$ cup vegetable oil
$1^1/_4$ cups water
4 eggs
2 cups white chocolate chips, divided
4 cups powdered sugar
$^1/_2$ cup butter, softened
sprinkles to garnish

What better to cozy up with on a cold winter day? All you need is a cup *of cocoa and a roaring fire and you're good to go. This cake is sure to* melt away your winter blues.

Preheat oven to 350° and grease a 10-inch Bundt pan. In mixing bowl, combine cake mix, pudding, oil, water, and eggs with electric mixer. Stir in one cup white chocolate chips. Pour into prepared pan and bake 40-45 minutes, or until toothpick inserted comes out clean. Let cake rest on counter in pan 10 minutes. Invert cake onto serving plate to finish cooling.

To make the frosting, first melt remaining cup white chocolate chips in microwave (stirring every 30 seconds). Then beat butter with powdered sugar and melted white chocolate until creamy. Spread on cooled cake and top with sprinkles.

TOASTED ALMOND

You know what makes a fancy bakery cake taste fancy? It's the almond extract. I promise.
A little almond adds that something special that makes this easy cake taste great.

INGREDIENTS

1 box white cake mix
2 small boxes instant vanilla pudding
$^1/_2$ cup vegetable oil
$1^1/_4$ cups water
4 eggs
$1^1/_2$ cups slivered almonds, toasted and
  divided (see below)
4 teaspoons almond extract, divided
4 cups powdered sugar
$^1/_2$ cup butter, softened
2-3 splashes milk

Preheat oven to 350° and grease a 10-inch Bundt pan. To toast almonds, put them in a dry pan over medium-high heat for about 5 minutes (stirring often).

In mixing bowl, combine cake mix, puddings, oil, water, and eggs with electric mixer. Stir in 1/2 cup toasted almonds and 2 teaspoons almond extract. Pour into prepared pan and bake 40-45 minutes, or until toothpick inserted comes out clean. Let cake rest on counter in pan 10 minutes. Invert the cake onto a serving plate to finish cooling.

Using an electric mixer, combine powdered sugar with butter and milk until you reach your desired frosting consistency. Stir in your remaining 2 teaspoons of almond extract. Frost cooled cake and garnish with your remaining toasted almonds.

MAPLE

I am a maple syrup snob. Once you have the real thing, you just can't go back.
And nothing makes me want pancakes and maple syrup more than a cold winter day.
This cake is a little piece of maple frosted goodness.

INGREDIENTS

1 box yellow cake mix
2 small boxes instant vanilla pudding
$^1/_2$ cup vegetable oil
$1^1/_4$ cups water
4 eggs
1 cup maple syrup, divided
4 cups powdered sugar
$^1/_2$ cup butter, softened
2-3 splashes milk

Preheat oven to 350° and grease a 10-inch Bundt pan. In mixing bowl, combine cake mix, puddings, oil, water, and eggs with electric mixer. Pour into prepared pan and bake 40-45 minutes, or until toothpick inserted comes out clean. Let cake rest on counter in pan 10 minutes. Invert the cake onto a serving plate to finish cooling. While the cake is still warm, take the end of a wooden spoon and poke holes across the top of your cake (visualize each piece you're cutting having one hole in it, so about 14 or so holes). Drizzle about $^3/_4$ cup maple syrup over the top of the cake and into the holes. Let the cake finish cooling.

To make the maple frosting, use an electric mixer and combine powdered sugar with butter, milk, and remaining $^1/_4$ cup syrup until you reach your desired frosting consistency. Add more powdered sugar if it's too thin and more milk if it's too thick. Frost cooled cake.

PECAN STREUSEL COFFEE CAKE

INGREDIENTS

1 box yellow cake mix
2 small boxes instant vanilla pudding
½ cup vegetable oil
1¼ cups water
4 eggs
2 tablespoons cinnamon, divided
¼ cup brown sugar
½ cup pecans, chopped
powdered sugar for dusting

*This is my take on
a classic coffee cake.*

Preheat oven to 350° and grease a 10-inch Bundt pan. In mixing bowl, combine cake mix, puddings, oil, water, eggs, and one tablespoon cinnamon with electric mixer. Set aside. In another smaller bowl, combine remaining tablespoon cinnamon, brown sugar, and pecans. Pour half the batter into prepared pan. Take your brown sugar mixture and sprinkle over batter. Pour remaining half of the batter over brown sugar layer and bake 40-45 minutes, or until toothpick inserted comes out clean. Let cake rest on counter in pan 10 minutes. Invert cake onto serving plate to finish cooling. Dust with powdered sugar after cake has finished cooling.

VANILLA LATTE

I'm meshing my two favorite things: cake and lattes.
Seriously. I've made many a meal out of cake and a latte. This is my kind of food!

INGREDIENTS

1 box white cake mix
2 small boxes instant vanilla pudding
$\frac{1}{2}$ cup vegetable oil
$1\frac{1}{4}$ cups water
4 eggs
2 vanilla beans split and seeds removed
4 cups powdered sugar
$\frac{1}{2}$ cup butter, softened
3-4 splashes brewed coffee, cooled to room temp
1 teaspoon vanilla extract

Preheat oven to 350° and grease a 10-inch Bundt pan. In mixing bowl, combine cake mix, puddings, oil, water, and eggs with electric mixer. Stir in seeds from your vanilla beans. Pour batter into prepared pan and bake 40-45 minutes, or until toothpick inserted comes out clean. Let cake rest on counter in pan 10 minutes. Invert cake onto serving plate to finish cooling.

To make the frosting, beat butter with powdered sugar and coffee until creamy. Stir in vanilla extract. Spread on cooled cake.

CHOCOLATE CHIP AND BOURBON

A little bourbon, a little chocolate,
a lot of flavor, all in one cake.

INGREDIENTS

1 box yellow cake mix
2 small boxes instant vanilla pudding
$1/2$ cup vegetable oil
$3/4$ cup water
$1/2$ cup bourbon
4 eggs
1 cup chocolate chips
$1/2$ cup butter, softened
4 cups powdered sugar
2-3 splashes milk
1 teaspoon vanilla

Preheat oven to 350° and grease a 10-inch Bundt pan. In mixing bowl, combine cake mix, puddings, oil, water, $1/2$ cup bourbon, and eggs with electric mixer. Stir in chocolate chips. Pour into prepared pan and bake 40-45 minutes, or until toothpick inserted comes out clean. Let cake rest on counter in pan 10 minutes. Invert the cake onto a serving plate to finish cooling.

To make your frosting, beat your butter, powdered sugar, milk, and vanilla with an electric mixer. Add more milk if the frosting is too thick and more powdered sugar if it's too thin. Frost cooled cake.

STICKY TOFFEE

INGREDIENTS

1 box yellow cake mix
2 small boxes instant vanilla pudding
$^1/_2$ cup vegetable oil
$1^1/_4$ cups water
4 eggs
1 cup Heath Pieces (find them in the
   chocolate chip aisle)
1 tablespoon light corn syrup
$^1/_4$ cup butter
$^1/_4$ cup dark brown sugar

$^1/_4$ cup sugar
$^1/_3$ cup half-and-half or heavy whipping cream
1 teaspoon vanilla

*I try not to play favorites with
my cakes, but this one is easily
in my top three.*

Preheat oven to 350° and grease a 10-inch Bundt pan. In mixing bowl, combine cake mix, puddings, oil, water, and eggs with electric mixer. Stir in Heath Pieces. Pour into prepared Bundt pan. Bake 40-45 minutes, or until toothpick inserted comes out clean. Let cake rest on counter in pan 10 minutes. Invert cake onto serving plate to finish cooling.

While the cake is cooling, prepare your toffee sauce. In a small saucepan over medium-high heat, melt your corn syrup, butter, brown sugar, and sugar, stirring constantly for about 4 minutes or until bubbly. Add in your half-and-half and vanilla and continue to stir another 2 minutes. Remove from heat and set aside to cool about 5 minutes. Poor warm toffee sauce over cooled cake.

ORANGE POPPY SEED

This cake is light and fresh with a little kick of orange. It's just the cure for a cold winter day but would also be delicious by the pool during the heat of summer.

INGREDIENTS

1 box yellow cake mix
2 small boxes instant vanilla pudding
½ cup vegetable oil
1¼ cups water
4 eggs
2 tablespoons poppy seeds
1 large orange
2 cups powdered sugar

Preheat oven to 350° and grease a 10-inch Bundt pan. In mixing bowl, combine cake mix, puddings, oil, water, and eggs with electric mixer. Stir in poppy seeds. Zest the orange and juice it. Stir half the zest and half the juice into the batter, reserving the remaining zest and juice. Pour into prepared pan and bake 40-45 minutes, or until toothpick inserted comes out clean. Let cake rest on counter in pan 10 minutes. Invert cake onto serving plate to finish cooling.

To make the glaze, combine powdered sugar with remaining orange zest and juice. Add more powdered sugar if your glaze is too runny or a little milk if it's too thick. Spoon over cooled cake.

SALTED CARAMEL MOCHA

Salt is a dessert's best friend. It draws out the sweetness and makes chocolate and caramel taste even better.

INGREDIENTS

1 box chocolate cake mix
2 small boxes instant chocolate pudding
$\frac{1}{2}$ cup vegetable oil
$1\frac{1}{4}$ cups water, *hot*
1 tablespoon instant coffee
4 eggs
1 cup caramel pieces
1 cup butter, softened
1 teaspoon vanilla
$\frac{1}{2}$ cup caramel ice cream topping
1 teaspoon sea salt, plus a pinch more for garnish
4 cups powdered sugar
3-4 splashes of milk

Preheat oven to 350° and grease a 10-inch Bundt pan. Start by heating the water in the microwave for two minutes—it needs to be hot. Stir in instant coffee to dissolve.

In mixing bowl, combine cake mix, puddings, oil, coffee water, and eggs with electric mixer. Stir in caramel pieces. Pour into prepared Bundt pan. Bake 40-45 minutes, or until toothpick inserted comes out clean. Let cake rest on counter in pan 10 minutes. Invert cake onto serving plate to finish cooling.

To make the frosting, beat butter and vanilla with electric mixer until smooth, then beat in caramel topping and salt. Slowly beat in powdered sugar and milk until frosting reaches desired consistency. Frost cake and garnish with a pinch more salt and a drizzle of caramel topping.

MARBLE

INGREDIENTS

1 box yellow cake mix
2 small boxes instant vanilla pudding
½ cup vegetable oil
1¼ cups water
4 eggs
1 cup chocolate chips, melted

A yellow and chocolate marble cake is the best of both worlds all swirled together. I kept my cake unfrosted, but of course you could add a variety of yummy frostings to the top. Simple, delicious, and sure to satisfy both the chocolate and yellow cake lover in your family.

Preheat oven to 350° and grease a 10-inch Bundt pan. In mixing bowl, combine cake mix, puddings, oil, water, and eggs with electric mixer. Pour two-thirds of the batter into prepared pan. Take your melted chocolate chips and beat them into the remaining one-third of the batter. Pour the chocolate batter on top of the yellow batter. Taking a knife, gently swirl the two batters together inside the Bundt pan. (Be careful not to swirl them too much.) Bake 40-45 minutes, or until toothpick inserted comes out clean. Let cake rest on counter in pan 10 minutes. Invert cake onto serving plate to finish cooling.

Valentine's Day

WHITE CHOCOLATE RASPBERRY

INGREDIENTS

1 box white cake mix
2 small boxes instant white chocolate pudding
   (use vanilla if you can't find white chocolate)
$^1/_2$ cup vegetable oil
$1^1/_4$ cups water
4 eggs
$1^1/_2$ cups white chocolate chips, divided
1 cup raspberry jam
4 cups powdered sugar
$^1/_2$ cup butter, softened
$^1/_4$ cup fresh raspberries, plus extra to garnish

White Chocolate Raspberry just sounds fancy, right? The perfect cake for a romantic evening. I usually spend my evenings with my favorite kiddos and my main man, and then I'm asleep by ten o'clock. Maybe after the kids are in bed, you and your love can have a piece? The fresh raspberries make the frosting extra delicious. And that layer of raspberry jam? Perfection!

Preheat oven to 350° and grease a 10-inch Bundt pan. In mixing bowl, combine cake mix, puddings, oil, water, and eggs with electric mixer. Stir in one cup white chocolate chips. Pour half of the batter into prepared pan, take your jam, and spread it over the batter in the pan. Pour remaining half of the batter over jam and bake 40-45 minutes, or until toothpick inserted comes out clean. Let cake rest on counter in pan 10 minutes. Invert cake onto serving plate to finish cooling.

Meanwhile, melt remaining $^1/_2$ cup white chocolate chips in the microwave (stirring every 30 seconds). To make the frosting, beat butter with powdered sugar, melted white chocolate, and fresh raspberries until creamy. Add more powdered sugar if your icing is too runny and a few more raspberries if it's too thick. Spread on cooled cake and top with fresh raspberries.

CHOCOLATE TRES LECHES

Doesn't a Chocolate Tres Leches cake sound romantic? Like it would be perfect for Valentine's Day? This cake uses **three kinds of milk** *to make it* **extra moist and delicious.** *I thought chocolate would add an even more romantic element to this cake.*

INGREDIENTS

1 box chocolate cake mix
2 small boxes instant chocolate pudding
$\frac{1}{2}$ cup vegetable oil
1 cup water
$\frac{1}{4}$ cup milk
4 eggs
$\frac{1}{2}$ cup sweetened condensed milk
4 cups powdered sugar
$\frac{1}{2}$ cup butter, softened
2-3 splashes vanilla coffee creamer or milk
   (creamer gives the frosting a bit more flavor,
   but use milk if you don't have any)
$\frac{1}{4}$ cup caramel ice cream topping

Preheat oven to 350° and grease a 10-inch Bundt pan. In mixing bowl, combine cake mix, puddings, oil, water, milk, and eggs with electric mixer. Pour into pan and bake 40-45 minutes, or until toothpick comes out clean. Let cake rest on counter in pan 10 minutes. Invert the cake onto a serving plate to finish cooling.

While the cake is still warm, take the end of a wooden spoon and poke holes across the top of your cake (visualize each piece you're cutting having one hole in it, so about 14 or so holes). Drizzle sweetened condensed milk over the top of the cake and into the holes. Let the cake finish cooling.

To make the frosting, use an electric mixer and combine powdered sugar with butter, coffee creamer (or milk), and caramel until you reach your desired frosting consistency. Frost cooled cake.

CHOCOLATE-COVERED CHERRY

When I think of love, I always think of my parents. My mom always buys my dad chocolate-covered cherries for Valentine's Day. Cherry gelatin makes the cake a pretty red color *while also giving it a* nice cherry flavor.

INGREDIENTS

1 box white cake mix
2 small boxes instant cherry gelatin
$^{1}/_{2}$ cup vegetable oil
$1^{1}/_{4}$ cups water
4 eggs
1 container chocolate frosting

Preheat oven to 350° and grease a 10-inch Bundt pan. In mixing bowl, combine cake mix, gelatin, oil, water, and eggs with electric mixer. Pour into prepared Bundt pan.

Bake 40-45 minutes, or until toothpick inserted comes out clean. Let cake rest on counter in pan 10 minutes. Invert cake onto serving plate to finish cooling.

Frost cooled cake with your favorite chocolate frosting.

STRAWBERRY

INGREDIENTS

1 box strawberry cake mix
2 small boxes instant vanilla pudding
½ cup vegetable oil
1¼ cups frozen strawberries, thawed
4 eggs
1 container strawberry frosting

*Wouldn't a pink cake be perfect for
Valentine's Day? I think so!
This cake is extra flavorful because
I substitute strawberries for the water.
Enjoy a slice with your sweetie!*

Before we get started, let's chat about the strawberries. You buy the frozen kind but then thaw them for this recipe. When you pour the thawed berries into your measuring cup to get the correct amount, you'll get big chunks of strawberry in there too. That's fine! The strawberries will mix up in the batter and create great flavor and a little bit of texture.

Preheat oven to 350° and grease a 10-inch Bundt pan. In mixing bowl, combine cake mix, puddings, oil, strawberries, and eggs with electric mixer. Pour into prepared pan and bake about 50 minutes or until toothpick inserted comes out clean. Let cake rest on counter in pan 10 minutes. Invert cake onto serving plate to finish cooling.

Frost cooled cake with strawberry frosting.

WHITE CHOCOLATE MACADAMIA NUT

White chocolate and macadamia nuts are a perfect combination!
They are sweethearts. Bake this cake on Valentine's Day and share a piece with
your sweetheart. It's a match made in heaven.

INGREDIENTS

1 box white cake mix
2 small boxes instant vanilla pudding
$\frac{1}{2}$ cup vegetable oil
$1\frac{1}{4}$ cups water
4 eggs
1 cup white chocolate chips
$1\frac{1}{2}$ cups macadamia nuts, toasted and
    divided (see below)
1 container cream cheese frosting

Preheat oven to 350° and grease a 10-inch Bundt pan. To toast macadamia nuts, put them in a clean, dry pan over medium-high heat for about 5 minutes (stirring often). They'll brown up quickly, so don't look away.

In mixing bowl, combine cake mix, puddings, oil, water, and eggs with electric mixer. Stir in $\frac{3}{4}$ cup toasted macadamia nuts and white chocolate chips. Pour into prepared pan and bake 40-45 minutes, or until toothpick inserted comes out clean. Let cake rest on counter in pan 10 minutes. Invert the cake onto a serving plate to finish cooling.

Frost cooled cake with your cream cheese frosting and garnish with your remaining macadamia nuts.

PINK VELVET

This cake just says love. If you can't find pink food coloring,
use a little red. Your sweethearts will love their Pink Velvet.

INGREDIENTS

1 box white cake mix
2 small boxes instant vanilla pudding
$^1/_2$ cup vegetable oil
$1^1/_4$ cups water
4 eggs
pink food coloring
1 container cream cheese frosting
pink sprinkles

Preheat oven to 350° and grease a 10-inch Bundt pan or 12 mini Bundt pans.
In mixing bowl, combine cake mix, puddings, oil, water, and eggs with an electric mixer. Mix
in a few drops of pink food coloring. Pour into prepared Bundt pan. Bake 40-45 minutes for
a large cake or 16-18 minutes for mini cakes, or until toothpick inserted comes out clean. Let cake rest
on counter in pan 10 minutes. Invert cake onto serving plate to finish cooling.

Frost cooled cake with cream cheese frosting and add pink sprinkles.

DARK CHOCOLATE RASPBERRY

INGREDIENTS

1 box chocolate cake mix
2 small boxes instant chocolate pudding
½ cup vegetable oil
1¼ cups water
4 eggs
1 cup chocolate chips
1½ cups raspberry jam
4 cups powdered sugar
½ cup butter, softened
2 tablespoons dark chocolate cocoa powder

3-4 splashes of milk
1 teaspoon vanilla extract
fresh raspberries to garnish

Dark chocolate and raspberries?
Valentine's Day in a cake!

Preheat oven to 350° and grease a 10-inch Bundt pan. In mixing bowl, combine cake mix, puddings, oil, water, and eggs with electric mixer. Stir in one cup chocolate chips. Pour half the batter into prepared pan, take your jam, and spread it over the batter in the pan. Pour remaining half of the batter over jam and bake 40-45 minutes, or until toothpick inserted comes out clean. Let cake rest on counter in pan 10 minutes. Invert cake onto serving plate to finish cooling.

To make the frosting, beat butter with powdered sugar, cocoa powder, and milk until creamy. Stir in vanilla extract. Spread on cooled cake and top with fresh raspberries.

St. Patrick's Day

GRASSHOPPER

INGREDIENTS

1 box chocolate cake mix
2 small boxes instant chocolate pudding
$^{1}/_{2}$ cup vegetable oil
$1^{1}/_{4}$ cups water
4 eggs
2 teaspoons peppermint extract
1 container vanilla frosting
green food coloring

Grasshoppers, Thin Mints, Peppermint Patties...whatever you call them, chocolate and mint were meant to be together. And with a little green frosting, it's perfect for your St. Patrick's Day celebration.

Preheat oven to 350° and grease a 10-inch Bundt pan or 12 mini Bundt pans.

In mixing bowl, combine cake mix, puddings, oil, water, and eggs with an electric mixer. Mix in peppermint extract. Pour into prepared Bundt pan. Bake 40-45 minutes for a large cake or 16-18 minutes for mini cakes, or until toothpick inserted comes out clean. Let cake rest on counter in pan 10 minutes. Invert cake onto serving plate to finish cooling.

Add a few drops of green food coloring to your vanilla frosting (you could even add another teaspoon of peppermint extract if you really wanted your cake minty). Frost your cake(s) with green frosting.

IRISH CREAM

Nothing says St. Patrick's Day like Irish Cream!
I'm sure my Irish ancestors would be pretty proud of this cake.

INGREDIENTS

1 box yellow cake mix
2 small boxes instant vanilla pudding
½ cup vegetable oil
1¼ cups water
4 eggs
4 tablespoons Irish Cream coffee creamer (the
   liquid not powdered kind!), divided
2 cups powdered sugar

Preheat oven to 350° and grease a 10-inch Bundt pan. In mixing bowl, combine cake mix, puddings, oil, water, and eggs with electric mixer. Stir in two tablespoons coffee creamer. Pour into prepared pan and bake 40-45 minutes, or until toothpick inserted comes out clean. Let cake rest on counter in pan 10 minutes. Invert cake onto serving plate to finish cooling.

To make the glaze, combine powdered sugar with remaining 2 tablespoons coffee creamer. Add more powdered sugar if your glaze is too runny or more creamer if it's too thick. Spoon over cooled cake.

PISTACHIO

Being the Irish girl that I am, I love me some St. Paddy's Day!
Two pistachio pudding mixes are all it takes to turn this basic white cake into
Irish green heaven. You and your lads and lassies will love it!

INGREDIENTS

1 box white cake mix
2 small boxes instant pistachio pudding
$\frac{1}{2}$ cup vegetable oil
$1\frac{1}{4}$ cups water
4 eggs
1 container vanilla frosting
green sprinkles to garnish

Preheat oven to 350° and grease a 10-inch Bundt pan. In mixing bowl, combine cake mix, puddings, oil, water, and eggs with electric mixer. Pour into prepared pan and bake 40-45 minutes, or until toothpick inserted comes out clean. Let cake rest on counter in pan 10 minutes. Invert the cake onto a serving plate to finish cooling.

Once the cake is cool, frost with vanilla frosting and add green sprinkles.

MINT CHOCOLATE OREO

INGREDIENTS

- 1 box chocolate cake mix
- 2 small boxes instant chocolate pudding
- $\frac{1}{2}$ cup vegetable oil
- $1\frac{1}{4}$ cups water
- 4 eggs
- 1 cup chocolate chips
- 4 cups powdered sugar
- $\frac{1}{2}$ cup butter, softened
- 3-4 splashes of milk (or peppermint mocha coffee creamer)
- 2 cups mint Oreos, crushed

You need a green cake for St. Patrick's Day, right? What's the best kind of green? Mint Oreos. But wait...You don't groove on the mint Oreos? Then replace them with regular crushed Oreos. Or peanut butter Oreos. Or strawberry milkshake Oreos. Mix and match!

Preheat oven to 350° and grease a 10-inch Bundt pan. In mixing bowl, combine cake mix, puddings, oil, water, and eggs with electric mixer. Stir in chocolate chips and pour into prepared Bundt pan. Bake 40-45 minutes, or until toothpick inserted comes out clean. Let cake rest on counter in pan 10 minutes. Invert cake onto serving plate to finish cooling.

To make the frosting, beat butter with powdered sugar and milk (or creamer) until creamy. Stir in crushed Oreo pieces. Spread on cooled cake.

CADBURY CREME EGG

INGREDIENTS

1 box chocolate cake mix
2 small boxes instant chocolate pudding
½ cup vegetable oil
1¼ cups water
4 eggs
7 Cadbury Creme Eggs (regular sized, not mini), roughly chopped
4 cups powdered sugar
½ cup butter, softened
3-4 splashes milk
1 teaspoon vanilla extract

I have fond memories of coming home to find that my mom had bought me Cadbury Creme Eggs. Who cares about Peeps? Who needs jelly beans? The only Easter candy that truly makes me happy is the creamy goodness of a Cadbury Creme Egg. This cake just makes sense at Easter time.

Preheat oven to 350° and grease a 10-inch Bundt pan. In mixing bowl, combine cake mix, puddings, oil, water, and eggs with electric mixer. Stir in 4 of your chopped Cadbury Creme Eggs. Pour batter into prepared pan and bake 40-45 minutes, or until toothpick inserted comes out clean. Let cake rest on counter in pan 10 minutes. Invert cake onto serving plate to finish cooling.

To make the frosting, beat butter with powdered sugar and milk until creamy. Stir in vanilla extract. Spread on cooled cake. Top with remaining 3 chopped Cadbury Creme Eggs.

CARROT

I just love me a piece of carrot cake with cream cheese frosting for Easter. I made my frosting from scratch (which is a cinch!) but of course, you could just spread on a store-bought frosting instead. Either way, nothing says Easter bunny like a piece of carrot cake.

INGREDIENTS

1 box carrot cake mix
2 small boxes instant vanilla pudding
$\frac{1}{2}$ cup vegetable oil
$1\frac{1}{4}$ cups water
4 eggs
1 cup pecans, chopped
4 cups powdered sugar
1 8-oz package cream cheese, softened
3-4 splashes milk
1 tablespoon vanilla

Preheat oven to 350° and grease a 10-inch Bundt pan. In mixing bowl, combine cake mix, puddings, oil, water, and eggs with electric mixer. Stir in pecan pieces. Pour into prepared pan and bake 40-45 minutes, or until toothpick inserted comes out clean.

Let cake rest on counter in pan 10 minutes. Invert cake onto serving plate to finish cooling.

To make the frosting, beat cream cheese with powdered sugar and a few splashes of milk until creamy. Stir in vanilla. Spread on cooled cake.

HAZELNUT CREAM

I like to do a white cake every Easter. And hey, who's to say you couldn't
throw a few jelly beans on top? It's your cake and your Easter. Go for it.

INGREDIENTS

1 box white cake mix
2 small boxes instant vanilla pudding
$^1/_2$ cup vegetable oil
$1^1/_4$ cups water
4 eggs
1 cup hazelnut coffee creamer, divided
1 container cream cheese frosting

Preheat oven to 350° and grease a 10-inch Bundt pan. In mixing bowl, combine cake mix, puddings, oil, water, and eggs with electric mixer. Pour into prepared pan and bake 40-45 minutes, or until toothpick inserted comes out clean. Let cake rest on counter in pan 10 minutes. Invert the cake onto a serving plate to finish cooling.

While the cake is still warm, take the handle end of a wooden spoon and poke holes all the way around the top of the cake (try and visualize one hole in each slice of cake, so about 14 holes). Drizzle all but 2 tablespoons hazelnut creamer over the top of the cake into the holes. Let your cake cool.

Take your store-bought cream cheese frosting and add 2 tablespoons of hazelnut creamer to it. Stir to incorporate. Frost your cooled cake with your hazelnut frosting. And perhaps top your cake with a few jelly beans!

CARROT AND ZUCCHINI

INGREDIENTS

1 box carrot cake mix (use spice cake if you
   can't find carrot cake)
2 small boxes instant vanilla pudding
$^1/_2$ cup vegetable oil
$1^1/_4$ cups water
4 eggs
$^1/_2$ cup grated carrots
$^1/_2$ cup grated zucchini
1 container cream cheese frosting
1 tablespoon cinnamon

Carrots and zucchini in your cake?
That's practically health food.

Preheat oven to 350° and grease a 10-inch Bundt pan or 12 mini Bundt pans.

In mixing bowl, combine cake mix, puddings, oil, water, and eggs with an electric mixer. Stir in grated carrots and zucchini. Pour into prepared Bundt pan. Bake 40-45 minutes for a large cake or 16-18 minutes for mini cakes, or until toothpick inserted comes out clean. Let cake rest on counter in pan 10 minutes. Invert cake onto serving plate to finish cooling.

Stir cinnamon into your store-bought cream cheese frosting. Frost cooled cake with your cinnamon cream cheese frosting.

4th of July

RED, WHITE, AND BLUE

INGREDIENTS

1 box white cake mix
2 small boxes instant vanilla pudding
1/2 cup vegetable oil
1 1/4 cups water
4 eggs
2 containers vanilla frosting
red food coloring

blue food coloring
red, white, and blue sprinkles to garnish

The Fourth of July is a time to celebrate by the pool, watch fireworks, and grill out for dinner. But most importantly, it's a time to give thanks for our independence.

Preheat oven to 350° and grease a 10-inch Bundt pan. In mixing bowl, combine cake mix, puddings, oil, water, and eggs with electric mixer. Divide the batter between three bowls. In one bowl, add 7-8 drops of red food coloring and stir. In the second bowl, add 4-5 drops of blue food coloring and stir. Don't add anything to the third bowl.

Pour the red cake batter in the prepared Bundt pan first. Spread evenly over bottom of pan. Next, pour the white batter over the red and carefully spread it on top. Finally, pour the blue batter on top of the white. Bake 40-45 minutes, or until toothpick inserted comes out clean.

Let cake rest on counter in pan 10 minutes. Invert the cake onto a serving plate to finish cooling.

To make the frosting, divide both cans of frosting between three microwavable bowls. Microwave one bowl of white frosting for about 15 seconds. Drizzle frosting over entire cake. Next, microwave another bowl 15 seconds. After it's microwaved, stir in a few drops of red food coloring. Drizzle red frosting over and around the white frosting. Finally, microwave the third bowl of frosting and then add in your blue food coloring. Drizzle the blue frosting over the red and white. Top with sprinkles.

RED, WHITE, AND BLUEBERRY

INGREDIENTS

1 box white cake mix
2 small boxes instant vanilla pudding
1/2 cup vegetable oil
1 1/4 cups water
4 eggs
1 cup fresh blueberries tossed with two
   tablespoons flour
1/2 cup butter, softened
3 cups powdered sugar

1-2 splashes of milk
1 cup fresh strawberries, chopped

*Celebrate this Fourth of July with
fireworks, watermelon, swimming,
and a slice of this fruity cake!*

Preheat oven to 350° and grease a 10-inch Bundt pan. In mixing bowl, combine cake mix, puddings, oil, water, and eggs with electric mixer. Stir in blueberries that have been tossed with flour. (This keeps the berries from sinking to the bottom of your cake.) Pour into prepared pan and bake 40-45 minutes, or until toothpick inserted comes out clean. Let cake rest on counter in pan 10 minutes. Invert cake onto serving plate to finish cooling.

To make the frosting, beat butter, powdered sugar, milk, and strawberries with an electric mixer. Add more powdered sugar if the frosting is too thin or more milk if it's too thick. Frost cooled cake.

CANDY CORN

INGREDIENTS

1 box white cake mix
2 small boxes instant vanilla pudding
½ cup vegetable oil
1¼ cups water
4 eggs
1 container vanilla frosting
3 teaspoons almond extract, divided
orange food coloring
yellow food coloring
candy corn to garnish

This cake looks fancy but it's simple to make. The key is the almond extract— it gives the cake a little something special. A delicious treat for your trick-or-treaters!

Preheat oven to 350° and grease a 10-inch Bundt pan. In mixing bowl, combine cake mix, puddings, oil, water, and eggs with electric mixer. Stir in 2 teaspoons almond extract.

Divide the batter between two bowls. In one bowl, add 7-8 drops of orange food coloring and stir. In the second bowl, add 7-8 drops of yellow food coloring and stir. Pour the orange cake batter in the prepared Bundt pan first. Spread out evenly over bottom of pan. Next, pour the yellow batter over the orange and carefully spread it on top. Bake 40-45 minutes, or until toothpick inserted comes out clean. Let cake rest on counter in pan 10 minutes. Invert the cake onto a serving plate to finish cooling.

To make the frosting, add one teaspoon of almond extract into your vanilla frosting and stir. Spread over cooled cake and top with candy corn.

CHOCOLATE COFFEE HAZELNUT

Nothing is better than a big piece of cake and a hot cup of coffee...thus, this cake. It turned out to be a **sophisticated twist** *on a Halloween cake too. The chocolate cake with the white glaze would look frightfully good on any Halloween table. It's also* **frightfully delicious!**

INGREDIENTS

1 box chocolate cake mix
2 small boxes instant chocolate pudding
$\frac{1}{2}$ cup vegetable oil
$1\frac{1}{4}$ cups brewed coffee, cooled
4 eggs
3 tablespoons hazelnut coffee creamer, divided
1 cup chocolate chips
2 cups powdered sugar

Preheat oven to 350° and grease a 10-inch Bundt pan. In mixing bowl, combine cake mix, puddings, oil, coffee, eggs, and 1 tablespoon creamer with electric mixer. Stir in chocolate chips. Pour into prepared Bundt pan. Bake 40-45 minutes, or until toothpick inserted comes out clean. Let cake rest on counter in pan 10 minutes. Invert cake onto serving plate to finish cooling.

To make the glaze, stir together powdered sugar and 2-3 splashes of creamer until combined. Drizzle glaze over cooled cake.

REESE'S PEANUT BUTTER CUP

When Halloween comes, my house is brimming with our family's favorite goodies.
This cake is inspired by the candy my husband loves most!

INGREDIENTS

1 box chocolate cake mix
2 small boxes instant chocolate pudding
$\frac{1}{2}$ cup vegetable oil
$1\frac{1}{4}$ cups water
4 eggs
1 cup Reese's peanut butter chips
$\frac{2}{3}$ cup butter, softened
4 cups powdered sugar
3-4 tablespoons milk
1 teaspoon vanilla
1 cup creamy peanut butter
Reese's Pieces to garnish

Preheat oven to 350° and grease a 10-inch Bundt pan or 12 mini Bundt pans.
In mixing bowl, combine cake mix, puddings, oil, water, and eggs with electric mixer. Add in Reese's chips and stir. Pour into prepared Bundt pan. Bake 40-45 minutes for a large cake or 16-18 minutes for mini cakes, or until toothpick inserted comes out clean. Let cake rest on counter in pan 10 minutes. Invert cake onto serving plate to finish cooling.

In a medium sized bowl, combine butter, powdered sugar, and milk with electric mixer until creamy. Add vanilla and peanut butter and beat until blended. Frost cooled cake and garnish with candy.

Thanksgiving

PECAN PIE

INGREDIENTS

1 box white cake mix
2 small boxes instant vanilla pudding
½ cup vegetable oil
1¼ cups water
4 eggs
2 tablespoons cinnamon
1 cup pecan pieces
1 cup caramel ice cream topping
½ cup butter, softened

4 cups powdered sugar
3-4 splashes milk (or pecan praline creamer)

My family would never have a Thanksgiving celebration without pecan pie. Ever! This cake is my tribute to the famous pie. A little pecan plus a gooey center.

Preheat oven to 350° and grease a 10-inch Bundt pan. In mixing bowl, combine cake mix, puddings, oil, water, eggs, and cinnamon with electric mixer. Stir in pecan pieces. Pour half of the batter into your prepared Bundt pan. Drizzle caramel over the batter in your pan and top with the remaining half of your cake batter. Bake 40-45 minutes, or until toothpick inserted comes out clean. Let cake rest on counter in pan 10 minutes. Invert cake onto serving plate to finish cooling.

To make the frosting, beat butter with powdered sugar and milk (or creamer) until creamy. Spread on cooled cake.

SWEET POTATO

INGREDIENTS

1 box spice cake mix
1 small box instant vanilla pudding
1 small box instant pumpkin spice pudding
(If unavailable, substitute another box vanilla
pudding and add 1 tablespoon cinnamon.)
1/2 cup vegetable oil
1 1/4 cups water
4 eggs
1 cup canned sweet potato, drained and mashed
1 tablespoon butter

1/4 cup sugar
1 container cream cheese frosting
1 cup chopped pecans, divided

*Instead of sweet potato pie this
Thanksgiving, make a sweet potato
Bundt cake. This super moist spice cake
is the perfect follow-up to your turkey.*

Preheat oven to 350° and grease a 10-inch Bundt pan. In mixing bowl, combine cake mix, puddings, oil, water, and eggs with electric mixer. Add in mashed sweet potatoes and mix until blended. Pour into prepared Bundt pan. Bake 40-45 minutes, or until toothpick inserted comes out clean. Let cake rest on counter in pan 10 minutes. Invert cake onto serving plate to finish cooling.

To make the praline crumbles on top, melt butter in saucepan over low heat, add sugar, and stir until sugar dissolves (it will become a caramel brown color). Add half a cup pecans and stir until coated. Pour praline mixture onto wax paper to cool (about 10 minutes). Break into pieces with hands. Use as garnish.

To assemble, put frosting in microwave-safe bowl and microwave 15 seconds (this gives it a creamier consistency for spreading). Add remaining half cup pecans. Stir until incorporated. Frost cake with pecan cream cheese frosting and top with praline crumbles.

Christmas

CHOCOLATE GINGERBREAD

INGREDIENTS

1 box chocolate cake mix
2 small boxes instant chocolate pudding
$\frac{1}{2}$ cup vegetable oil
$1\frac{1}{4}$ cups water
4 eggs
1 tablespoon plus 1 teaspoon ground ginger, divided
1 cup semisweet chocolate chips
2 cups powdered sugar
3-4 splashes milk

That's right—
chocolate and gingerbread
in one cake. Yummy!

Preheat oven to 350° and grease a 10-inch Bundt pan. In mixing bowl, combine cake mix, puddings, oil, water, eggs, and 1 tablespoon ginger with electric mixer. Add in chocolate chips. Pour into prepared Bundt pan. Bake 40-45 minutes, or until toothpick inserted comes out clean. Let cake rest on counter in pan 10 minutes. Invert cake onto serving plate to finish cooling.

To make the glaze, mix powdered sugar and remaining teaspoon ginger in a small bowl. Add in splashes of milk a little at a time, stirring until glaze reaches desired consistency. Drizzle over cooled cake.

EGGNOG

The eggnog makes this cake super, super moist.
What better way to celebrate Christmas?

INGREDIENTS

1 box yellow cake mix
2 small boxes instant vanilla pudding
½ cup vegetable oil
¾ cup eggnog
½ cup water
4 eggs
1 tablespoon rum extract, divided
1 tablespoon nutmeg, divided
1 container vanilla frosting

Preheat oven to 350° and grease a 10-inch Bundt pan or 12 mini Bundt pans.

In mixing bowl, combine cake mix, puddings, oil, eggnog, water, eggs, 2 teaspoons extract, and 1½ teaspoons nutmeg with electric mixer. Pour into prepared Bundt pan. Bake 40-45 minutes for a large cake or 16-18 minutes for mini cakes, or until toothpick inserted comes out clean. Let cake rest on counter in pan 10 minutes. Invert cake onto serving plate to finish cooling.

To make the frosting, stir remaining teaspoon of extract and remaining 1½ teaspoons nutmeg into the container of vanilla frosting. Frost and sprinkle with a little extra nutmeg for grins.

RED VELVET

Nothing is more festive at Christmas
than a red velvet cake!

INGREDIENTS

1 box red velvet cake mix
2 small boxes instant vanilla pudding
$1/2$ cup vegetable oil
$1^1/_4$ cups water
4 eggs
1 cup semisweet chocolate chips
1 8-oz. package cream cheese, softened
4 cups powdered sugar
3-4 splashes milk
red sprinkles, optional

Preheat oven to 350° and grease a 10-inch Bundt pan. In mixing bowl, combine cake mix, puddings, oil, water, and eggs with electric mixer. Add in chocolate chips. Pour into prepared Bundt pan. Bake 40-45 minutes, or until toothpick inserted comes out clean. Let cake rest on counter in pan 10 minutes. Invert cake onto serving plate to finish cooling.

To make the frosting, beat cream cheese with powdered sugar and milk until creamy. Spread on cooled cake and top with sprinkles.

VANILLA BEAN NOEL

INGREDIENTS

1 box white cake mix
2 small boxes instant vanilla pudding
½ cup vegetable oil
1¼ cups water
4 eggs
2 whole vanilla beans, seeds scraped
   from the inside
1 container vanilla frosting

May this cake
bring joy to your kitchen
in the holiday season.

Preheat oven to 350° and grease a 10-inch Bundt pan. In mixing bowl, combine cake mix, puddings, oil, water, and eggs with electric mixer. Add the seeds from one vanilla bean and beat until blended. Pour into prepared Bundt pan. Bake 40-45 minutes, or until toothpick inserted comes out clean. Let cake rest on counter in pan 10 minutes. Invert cake onto serving plate to finish cooling.

Pour frosting into a microwavable bowl and heat 15 seconds. Add the seeds from the remaining vanilla bean and stir until combined. Frost cake and enjoy!

CANDY CANE

This candy-cane striped cake is a huge crowd pleaser! Use crushed candy canes if you can't find peppermint crunch on the baking aisle.

INGREDIENTS

1 box white cake mix
2 small boxes instant vanilla pudding
½ cup vegetable oil
1¼ cups water
4 eggs
2 teaspoons peppermint extract, divided
red food coloring
4 cups powdered sugar
½ cup butter, softened
½ cup white chocolate chips, melted and cooled
peppermint crunch

Preheat oven to 350° and grease a 10-inch Bundt pan. In mixing bowl, combine cake mix, puddings, oil, water, and eggs with electric mixer. Divide batter into two bowls. Stir one teaspoon of peppermint extract and red food coloring in one bowl. Keep the other bowl plain. In your Bundt pan, spread the red layer across the bottom first (gently tap the pan against your counter once it's in to make sure everything is settled), then layer the white batter on top of the red. Bake 40-45 minutes, or until toothpick inserted comes out clean. Let cake rest on counter in pan 10 minutes. Invert cake onto serving plate to finish cooling.

To make the frosting, beat butter with powdered sugar and white chocolate until creamy. Stir in remaining teaspoon peppermint extract. Spread on cooled cake and top with peppermint crunch.

GINGERBREAD

One of my favorite things to do during the Christmas season is decorate a gingerbread house with my kiddos. The smell and flavor of gingerbread is almost magical. This cake is pretty magical too. You'll be singing "White Christmas" and eating a yummy cake in no time!

INGREDIENTS

1 box gingerbread cake mix
2 small boxes instant vanilla pudding
$\frac{1}{2}$ cup vegetable oil
$1\frac{1}{4}$ cups water
4 eggs
1 container cream cheese frosting

Preheat oven to 350° and grease a 10-inch Bundt pan. In mixing bowl, combine cake mix, puddings, oil, water, and eggs with electric mixer. Pour into prepared Bundt pan. Bake 40-45 minutes, or until toothpick inserted comes out clean. Let cake rest on counter in pan 10 minutes. Invert cake onto serving plate to finish cooling. Frost cooled cake with cream cheese frosting.

PEPPERMINT MOCHA

INGREDIENTS

- 1 box chocolate cake mix
- 2 small boxes instant chocolate pudding
- ½ cup vegetable oil
- ½ cup water
- ¾ cup brewed coffee, cooled
- 4 eggs
- 1 cup mint chocolate chips (or regular if you can't find them)
- 4 teaspoons peppermint extract, divided

- 1 container vanilla frosting
- 1 cup peppermint crunch, divided

Chocolate and peppermint:
Christmas perfection. This cake will get
you in the Jingle Bells mood in no time!

Preheat oven to 350° and grease a 10-inch Bundt pan. In mixing bowl, combine cake mix, puddings, oil, water, coffee, and eggs with electric mixer. Stir in chocolate chips and 2 teaspoons peppermint extract. Pour into prepared pan and bake 40-45 minutes, or until toothpick inserted comes out clean. Let cake rest on counter in pan 10 minutes. Invert cake onto serving plate to finish cooling.

To make the frosting, add remaining 2 teaspoons peppermint extract to vanilla frosting along with ½ cup peppermint crunch. Frost cooled cake and then garnish with remaining peppermint crunch.

PRALINE CINNAMON SPICE

During the holidays you can find cinnamon chips on the chocolate chip aisle.
They make this cake extra yummy, but if you can't find them, don't despair!
You can always substitute butterscotch chips.

INGREDIENTS

1 box spice cake mix
2 small boxes instant vanilla pudding
½ cup vegetable oil
1¼ cups water
4 eggs
⅓ cup cinnamon chips
2 cups praline pecans, divided
1 container cream cheese frosting

Preheat oven to 350° and grease a 10-inch Bundt pan. In mixing bowl, combine cake mix, puddings, oil, water, and eggs with electric mixer. Stir in cinnamon chips and one cup of praline pecans (break them up a bit). Pour into prepared Bundt pan. Bake 40-45 minutes, or until toothpick inserted comes out clean. Let cake rest on counter in pan 10 minutes. Invert cake onto serving plate to finish cooling. Frost cooled cake with cream cheese frosting and garnish with remaining praline pecans.

MISTLETOE MINT

Mistletoe and mint? That sounds like Christmas magic to me! These little cakes taste like the white chocolate and peppermint Hershey Kisses you find in stores this time of year. A little green just makes them more festive.

INGREDIENTS

1 box white cake mix
2 small boxes instant vanilla pudding
$1/2$ cup vegetable oil
$1^1/4$ cups water
4 eggs
4 teaspoons peppermint extract, divided
1 cup white chocolate chips
1 container vanilla frosting
green food coloring
red sprinkles

Preheat oven to 350° and grease a 10-inch Bundt pan or 12 mini Bundt pans.

In mixing bowl, combine cake mix, puddings, oil, water, eggs, and 2 teaspoons extract with electric mixer. Mix in a few drops of green food coloring. Stir in white chocolate chips. Pour into prepared Bundt pan. Bake 40-45 minutes for a large cake or 16-18 minutes for mini cakes, or until toothpick inserted comes out clean. Let cake rest on counter in pan 10 minutes. Invert cake onto serving plate to finish cooling.

To make the frosting, stir remaining 2 teaspoons of extract into the container of vanilla frosting along with a little green food coloring. Frost cake and add red sprinkles.

CHOCOLATE CARAMEL MACAROON

INGREDIENTS

1 box chocolate cake mix
2 small boxes instant coconut pudding
   (use chocolate if you can't find coconut)
$1/2$ cup vegetable oil
$1^1/4$ cups water
4 eggs
1 cup chocolate chips
1 jar caramel ice cream topping, divided
   4 cups sweetened coconut flakes, divided

$1/2$ cup butter, softened
4 cups powdered sugar
3-4 splashes milk

This cake looks really fancy but it is so simple to make. Simple fancy... That's a good recipe to have on hand during the holidays.

Preheat oven to 350° and grease a 10-inch Bundt pan. In mixing bowl, combine cake mix, puddings, oil, water, and eggs with electric mixer. Stir in chocolate chips. Pour half of your batter into prepared Bundt pan. Drop 8-10 tablespoons of caramel on top of batter all the way around the cake in the pan (it will spread out while baking). Top the caramel with a cup of coconut sprinkled around the pan. Pour remaining half of batter on top of your caramel and coconut layer. Bake 40-45 minutes, or until toothpick inserted comes out clean. Let cake rest on counter in pan 10 minutes. Invert cake onto serving plate to finish cooling.

Before you make your frosting, toast the remaining 3 cups of coconut. Place coconut in a dry skillet and toast over medium-high heat. Keep an eye on the coconut because after a few minutes it will start to brown. Toss in skillet about 6-7 minutes until nicely browned and toasted. Remove from heat and let it cool while you're preparing the frosting.

Using an electric mixer, beat butter, powdered sugar, and $1/2$ cup caramel topping with a few splashes of milk. Stir in one cup toasted coconut. Spread frosting over cooled cake and garnish with remaining 2 cups toasted coconut.

CRANBERRY ORANGE

For some reason, these two fruits are synonymous with the holiday season. Tart and flavorful, this cake will be the perfect accompaniment to any holiday gathering. From brunch to dinner, this cake has you covered.

INGREDIENTS

1 box yellow cake mix
2 small boxes instant vanilla pudding
½ cup vegetable oil
¾ cup water
½ cup fresh orange juice, plus more for glaze
4 eggs
3 tablespoons orange zest, divided
1 cup fresh cranberries
2 cups powdered sugar

Preheat oven to 350° and grease a 10-inch Bundt pan. In mixing bowl, combine cake mix, puddings, oil, water, orange juice, and eggs with electric mixer. Stir in 2 tablespoons of zest and cranberries. Pour into prepared pan and bake 40-45 minutes, or until toothpick inserted comes out clean. Let cake rest on counter in pan 10 minutes. Invert cake onto serving plate to finish cooling.

To make the glaze, combine powdered sugar with a tablespoon or two of fresh orange juice and remaining tablespoon of zest. Add more powdered sugar if your glaze is too runny or more juice if it's too thick. Spoon over cooled cake.

FRUIT CAKE

Let's face it: This is the Christmas cake. Songs are sung about it, it's given to practically everyone as a gift....it's synonymous with Christmas. And it's often disgusting, stale, dry, and just plain yucky. But just wait 'til you try this recipe!

INGREDIENTS

1 box yellow cake mix
2 small boxes instant vanilla pudding
$\frac{1}{2}$ cup vegetable oil
$1\frac{1}{4}$ cups water
4 eggs
1 tablespoon cinnamon
$\frac{1}{4}$ cup Maraschino cherries, chopped
$\frac{1}{4}$ cup dried pineapple
$\frac{1}{4}$ cup dried cranberries
$\frac{1}{4}$ cup dried apricots, chopped
2 cups powdered sugar
2-3 splashes milk

Preheat oven to 350° and grease a 10-inch Bundt pan. In mixing bowl, combine cake mix, puddings, oil, water, and eggs with electric mixer. Stir in cinnamon, cherries, pineapple, cranberries, and apricots. Pour into prepared pan and bake 40-45 minutes, or until toothpick inserted comes out clean. Let cake rest on counter in pan 10 minutes. Invert cake onto serving plate to finish cooling.

To make the glaze, combine powdered sugar with milk. Add more powdered sugar if your glaze is too runny or more milk if it's too thick. Spoon over cooled cake.

RED VELVET PEPPERMINT

INGREDIENTS

1 box red velvet cake mix
2 small boxes instant vanilla pudding
½ cup vegetable oil
1¼ cups water
4 eggs
1 8-oz. package cream cheese, softened
4 cups powdered sugar
3-4 splashes milk
1 teaspoon peppermint extract
crushed candy cane pieces to garnish

This cake is simple, moist, and totally tastes like Christmas! I think you should make it on Christmas Eve for the ones you love.

Preheat oven to 350° and grease a 10-inch Bundt pan or 12 mini Bundt pans.

In mixing bowl, combine cake mix, puddings, oil, water, and eggs with electric mixer. Pour into prepared Bundt pan. Bake 40-45 minutes for a large cake or 16-18 minutes for mini cakes, or until toothpick inserted comes out clean. Let cake rest on counter in pan 10 minutes. Invert cake onto serving plate to finish cooling.

To make the frosting, beat cream cheese with powdered sugar and milk until creamy. Beat in peppermint extract. Add more milk if your frosting is too thick and more powdered sugar if it's too thin. Spread on cooled cake and top with crushed candy cane pieces.

New Year's

PINK CHAMPAGNE

INGREDIENTS

1 box white cake mix
2 small boxes instant vanilla pudding
½ cup vegetable oil
1½ cups champagne, divided
4 eggs
4 cups powdered sugar
½ cup butter, softened
pink food coloring, optional
crystal sprinkles, optional

When I set out to create a cake with New Year's Eve in mind, my brain automatically went to champagne. It's festive, it's lively, it's a crowd pleaser...and so is this cake!

Preheat oven to 350° and grease a 10-inch Bundt pan. In mixing bowl, combine cake mix, puddings, oil, 1¼ cups champagne, and eggs with electric mixer. Stir in pink food coloring until batter reaches preferred pink color. Pour into prepared Bundt pan. Bake 40-45 minutes, or until toothpick inserted comes out clean. Let cake rest on counter in pan 10 minutes. Invert cake onto serving plate to finish cooling.

To make the frosting, beat butter with powdered sugar and remaining ¼ cup champagne until creamy. Stir in pink food coloring until desired pink color appears. Spread on cooled cake and top with sprinkles.

CELEBRATION WHITE

INGREDIENTS

1 box white cake mix
2 small boxes instant vanilla pudding
½ cup vegetable oil
1¼ cups water
4 eggs
3 teaspoons almond extract, divided
1 container vanilla frosting
sprinkles, optional

My favorite kind of cake is a piece of birthday or wedding cake. This is the **cake you make** *for special occasions!*

Preheat oven to 350° and grease a 10-inch Bundt pan. In mixing bowl, combine cake mix, puddings, oil, water, and eggs with electric mixer. Add in 2 teaspoons almond extract and beat until blended. Pour into prepared Bundt pan. Bake 40-45 minutes, or until toothpick inserted comes out clean. Let cake rest on counter in pan 10 minutes. Invert cake onto serving plate to finish cooling.

To make the frosting, pour remaining teaspoon of almond extract into your frosting. Stir until incorporated. Frost cooled cake.

101 CAKES LATER...

Making these Bundt cakes started out as a silly goal, but it ended up changing my life. For more than two years I stood in my kitchen with my oldest daughter, and we not only poured, stirred, baked, and frosted...but we talked, laughed, learned, and loved. Some of these cakes were for holidays, some were for celebratory days, and some were for just plain normal days, but they were all special because we made them together. Baking a cake doesn't have to be hard, and it doesn't have to take a lot of time or work. It just needs to be made with love and then shared with someone you adore.

Share your creations using #mixandmatchcakes!

INDEX OF RECIPES

Irish Cream, 110

Italian Cream, 16

Key Lime, 59

Lemon, 24

Lemon Cookie Crunch, 29

Maple, 85

Marble, 94

Margarita, 39

Mint Chocolate Oreo, 113

Mississippi Mud, 44

Mistletoe Mint, 143

Nutella, 17

Orange Poppy Seed, 92

Oreo, 15

Original Chocolate Chip, 9

Peach, 38

Peach Upside-Down, 55

Peanut Butter, 63

Peanut Butter and Banana, 21

Pecan Pie, 129

Pecan Streusel Coffee Cake, 86

Peppermint Mocha, 140

Piña Colada, 32

Pineapple Upside-Down, 51

Pink Champagne, 151

Pink Lemonade, 34

Pink Velvet, 105

Pistachio, 111

Praline Cinnamon Spice, 142

Pumpkin, 78

Pumpkin Spice Latte, 61

Rainbow, 58

Red Velvet, 135

Red Velvet Peppermint, 149

Red, White, and Blue, 121

Red, White, and Blueberry, 123

Reese's Peanut Butter Cup, 127

Root Beer, 50

S'mores, 71

Salted Caramel Mocha, 93

Snickerdoodle, 74

Sticky Toffee, 91

Strawberry, 103

Strawberry Coconut, 41

Strawberry Lemonade, 43

Sweet Potato, 130

Toasted Almond, 84

Toffee Crunch, 73

Vanilla Bean Noel, 137

Vanilla Latte, 88

White Chocolate Macadamia Nut, 104

White Chocolate Raspberry, 99

Winter White Chocolate, 83

SHAY SHULL

is the author of the *Mix and Match Mama* blog. Daily, she writes about motherhood, adoption, world travel, holidays, organization, and, of course, yummy food. Passionate about coffee, traveling the world with her family, and Red Sox baseball, her greatest love is Christ. Shay lives in McKinney, Texas, with her husband, Andrew, and their three kids, Kensington, Smith, and Ashby.

Follow Shay on social media as @MixandMatchMama.

To learn more about Harvest House books and
to read sample chapters, visit our website:

www.harvesthousepublishers.com

HARVEST HOUSE PUBLISHERS
EUGENE, OREGON